Volume 8

Series created by Terri Minsky

Gordo and the Girl
written by Melissa Gould

You're a Good Man, Lizzie McGuire

written by Allison Taylor

TOKYOPOP®

HAMBURG · LONDON · LOS ANGELES · TOKYO

Contributing Editors - Robert Buscemi & Amy Court Kaemon
Graphic Design & Lettering - Yolanda Petriz
Cover Layout - Patrick Hook
Additional Layout - Tomás Montalvo-Lagos &
Jennifer Nunn-Iwai

Editor - Erin Stein
Digital Imaging Manager - Chris Buford
Pre-Press Manager - Antonio DePietro
Production Managers - Jennifer Miller, Mutsumi Miyazaki
Art Director - Matt Alford
Managing Editor - Jill Freshney
VP of Production - Ron Klamert
President & C.O.O. - John Parker
Publisher & C.E.O. - Stuart Levy

E-mail: info@tokyopop.com
Come visit us online at www.TOKYOPOP.com

A  Cine-Manga® Book
TOKYOPOP Inc.
5900 Wilshire Blvd., Suite 2000, Los Angeles, CA 90036

LIZZIE MCGUIRE VOLUME 8

ISBN: 1-59532-279-5

First TOKYOPOP printing: October 2004

10 9 8 7 6 5 4 3 2

Printed in the USA

Lizzie McGuire

Volume 8

CONTENTS

LIZZIE McGUIRE:

A typical 14-year-old girl who has her fair share of bad hair days and embarrassing moments. Luckily, Lizzie knows how to admit when she's wrong, back up her friends and stand up for herself.

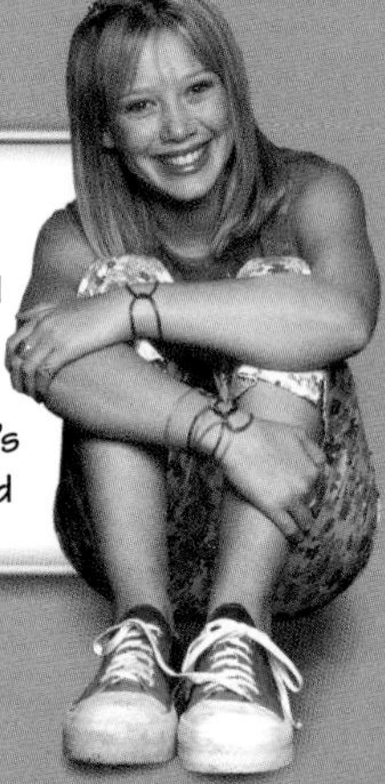

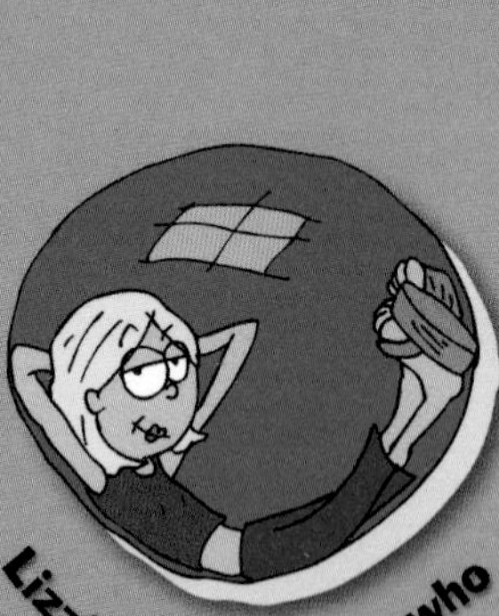

Lizzie's alter-ego, who says and does all the things Lizzie's afraid to.

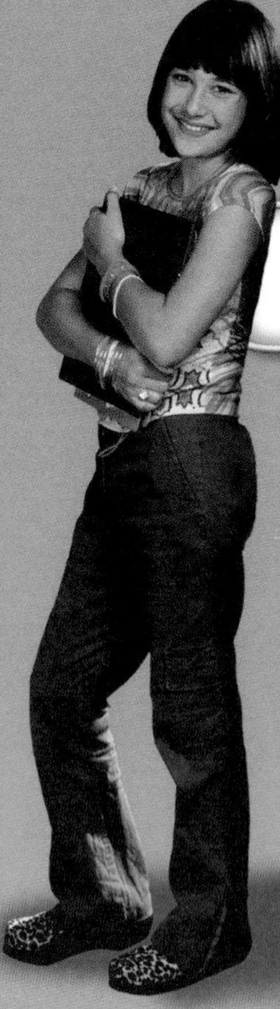

MIRANDA:

Lizzie's best friend.

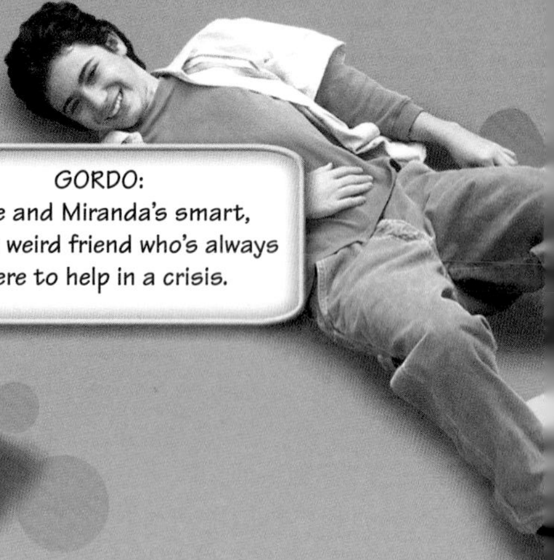

GORDO:

Lizzie and Miranda's smart, slightly weird friend who's always there to help in a crisis.

CHARACTER BIOS

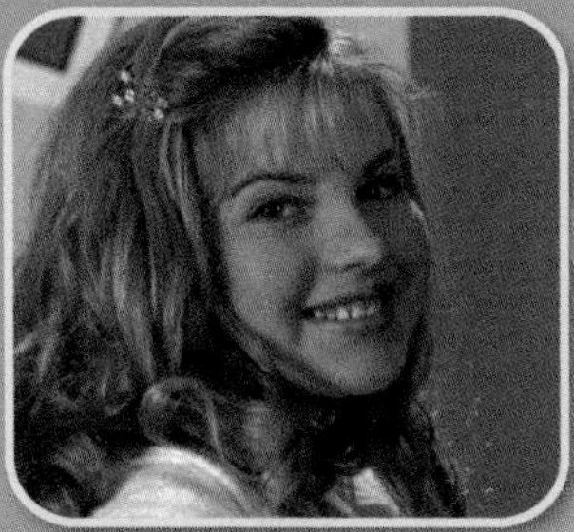

KATE:
Lizzie and Miranda's ex-friend who thinks she is too good for them now that she wears a bra.

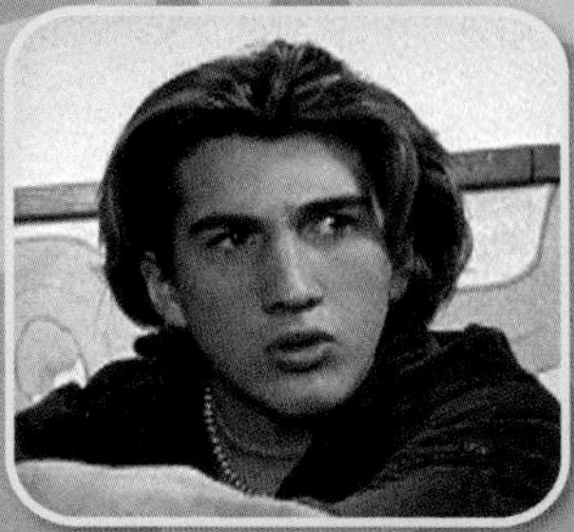

ETHAN:
The most popular guy in school.

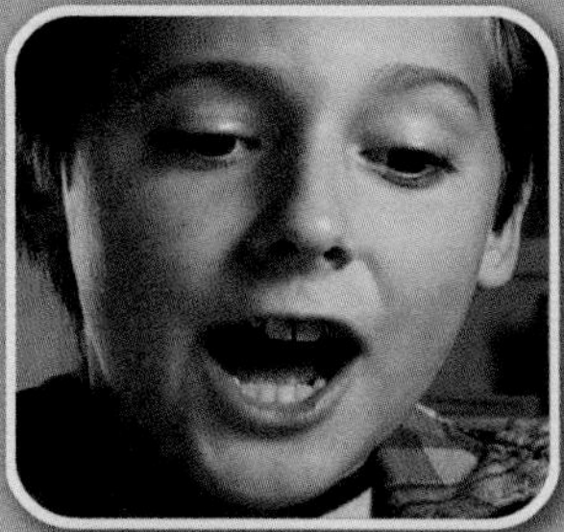

MATT:
Lizzie's little brother, who spends most of his time driving her crazy.

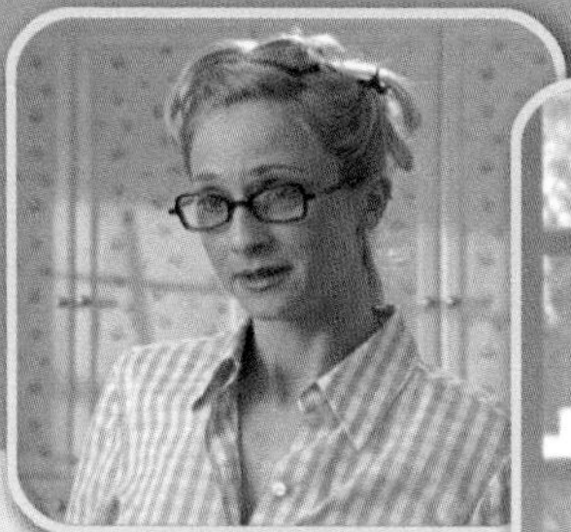

LIZZIE'S MOM:
She only wants the best for Lizzie, but sometimes she tries a little too hard.

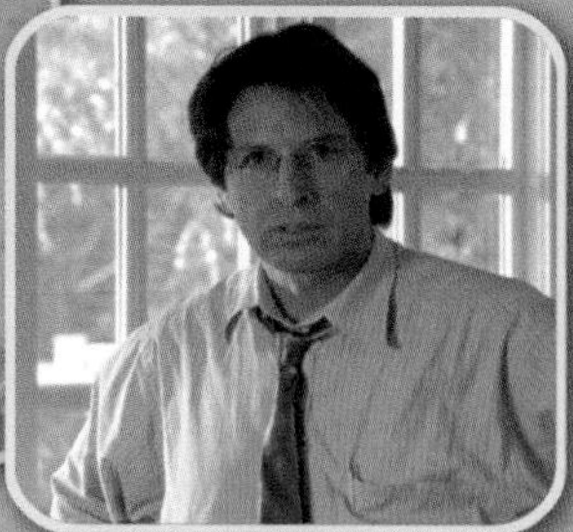

LIZZIE'S DAD:
He loves Lizzie, though he doesn't always know how to relate to her.

Lizzie McGuire

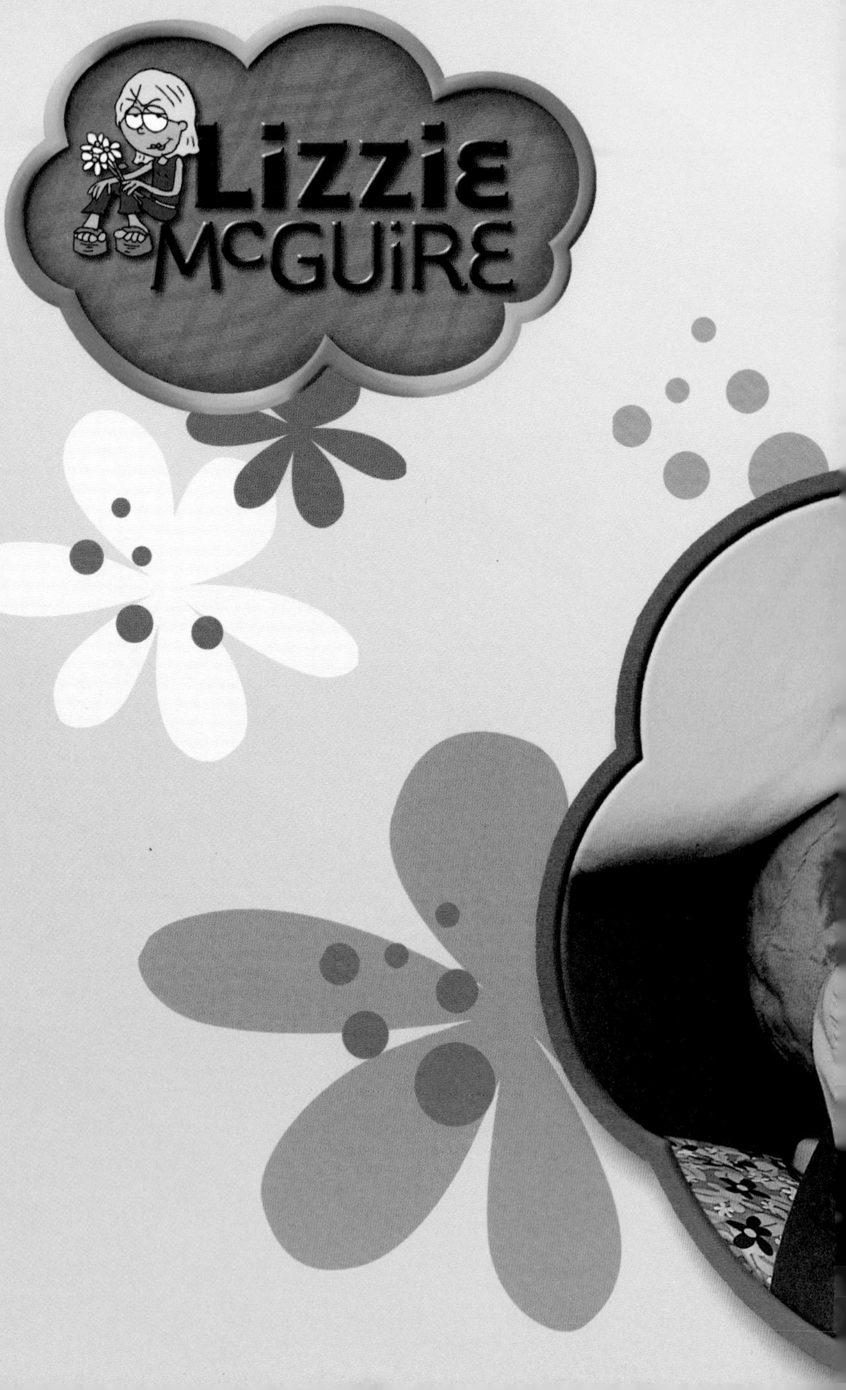

Gordo and the Girl

Gordo's got a girlfriend and Lizzie doesn't know what to do! But is spying on her best bud really the answer?

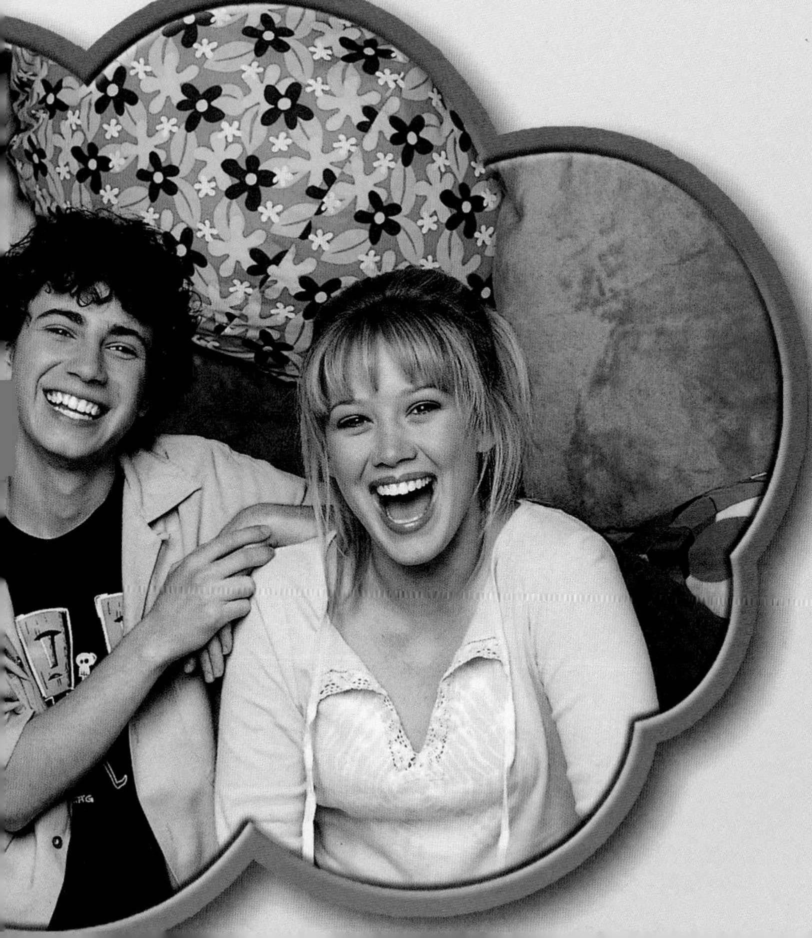

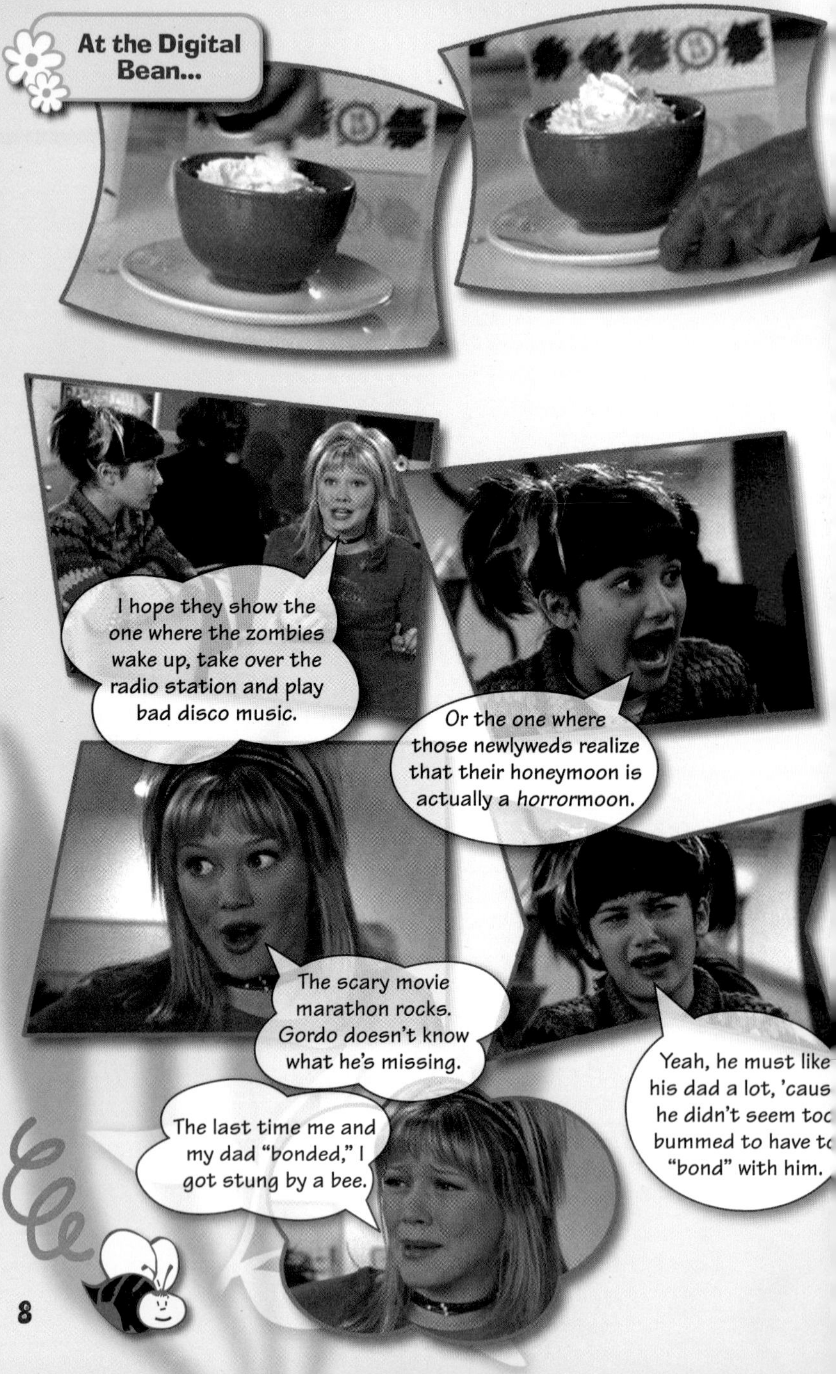

At the Digital Bean...
I hope they show the one where the zombies wake up, take over the radio station and play bad disco music.
Or the one where those newlyweds realize that their honeymoon is actually a *horrormoon*.
The scary movie marathon rocks. Gordo doesn't know what he's missing.
Yeah, he must like his dad a lot, 'caus he didn't seem to bummed to have t "bond" with him.
The last time me and my dad "bonded," I got stung by a bee.

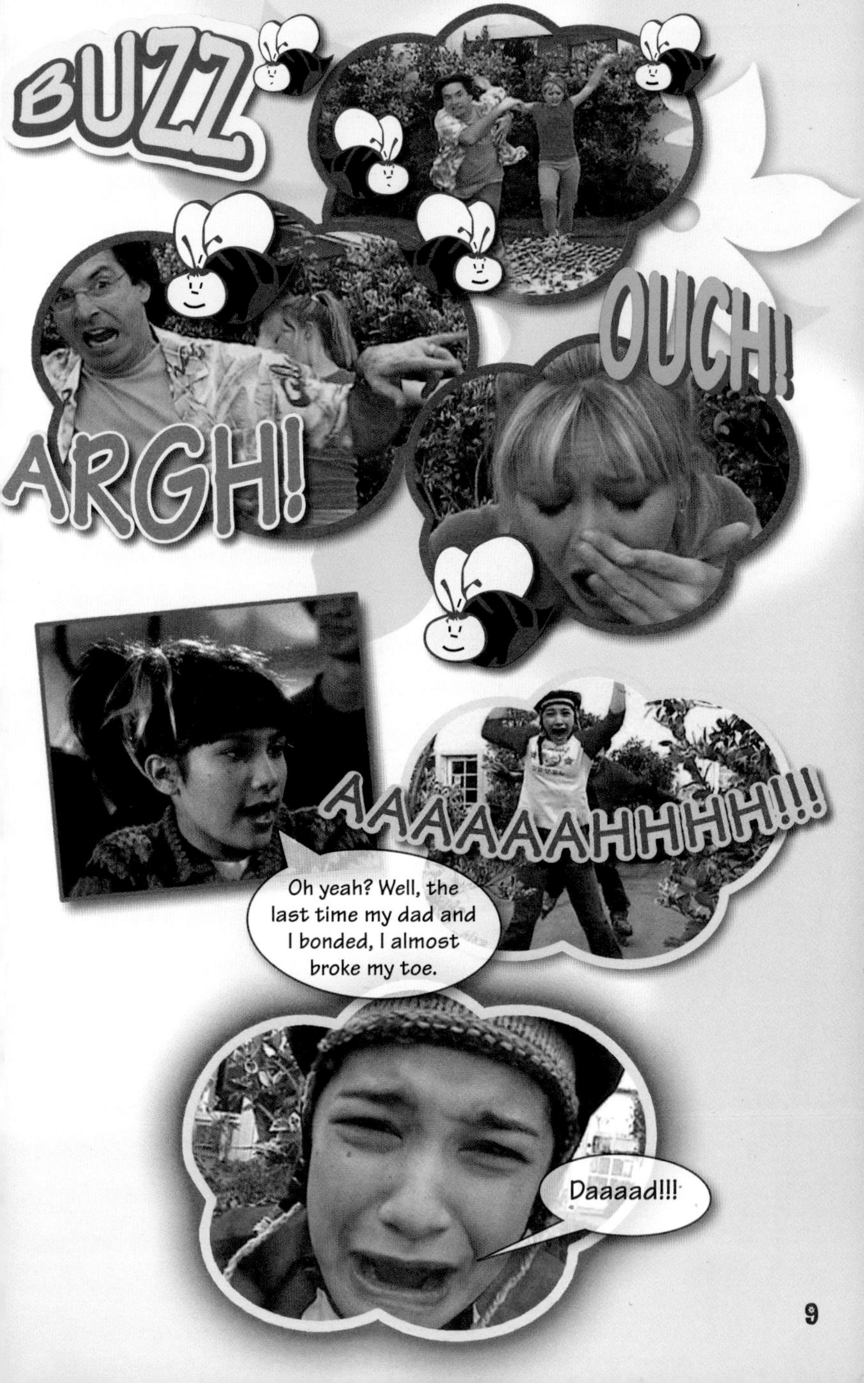
BUZZ
OUCH!
ARGH!
AAAAAAHHHH!!!
Oh yeah? Well, the last time my dad and I bonded, I almost broke my toe.
Daaaad!!!

Yup.
I think it's much safer staying at home and getting scared out of our brains.
Uh...are Gordo's dad and Brooke Baker the same person?
Huh?
GASP!
He and his dad must've rescheduled.
He obviously came here looking for us.

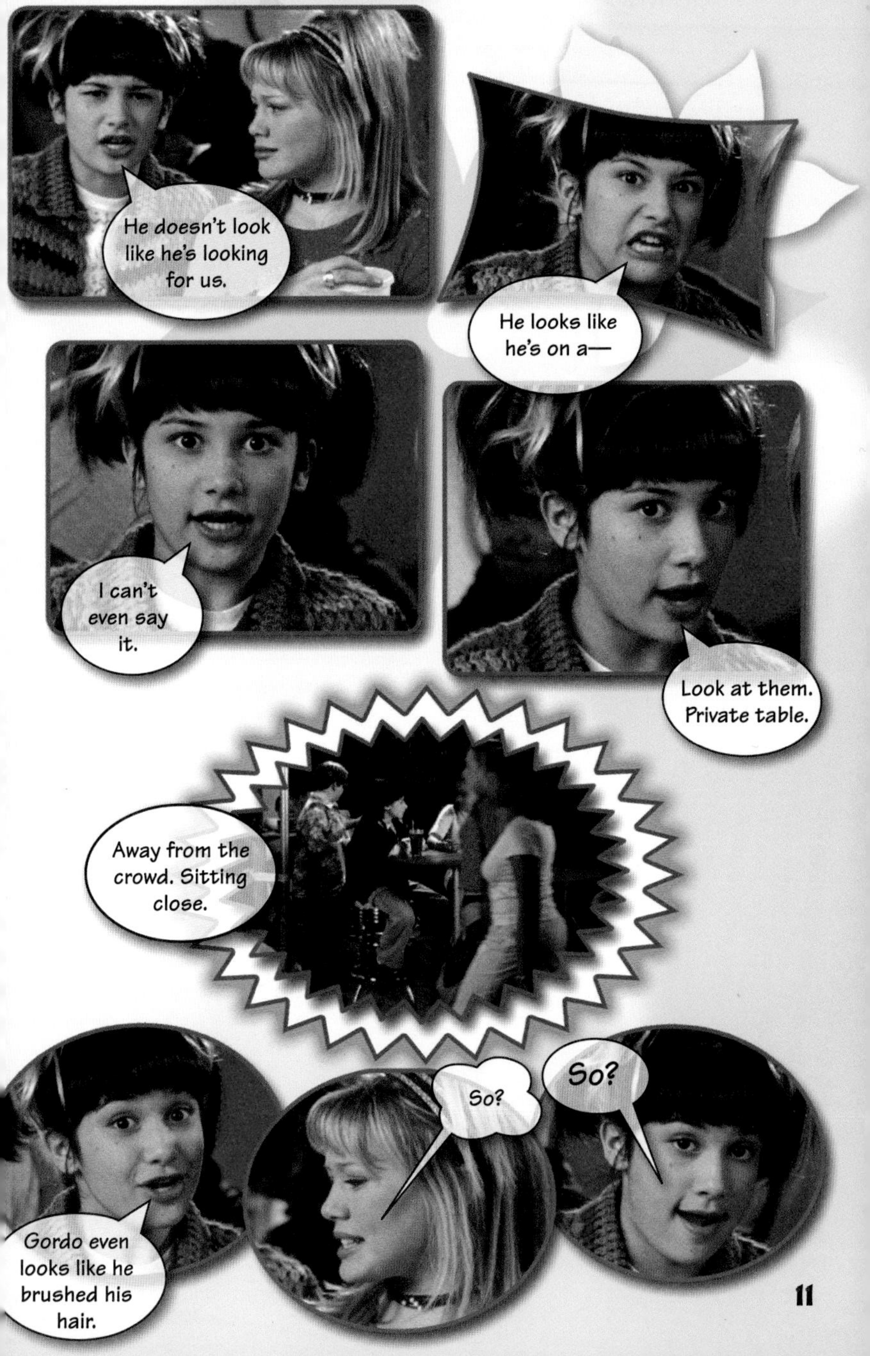
He doesn't look like he's looking for us.
He looks like he's on a—
I can't even say it.
Look at them. Private table.
Away from the crowd. Sitting close.
Gordo even looks like he brushed his hair.
So?
So?

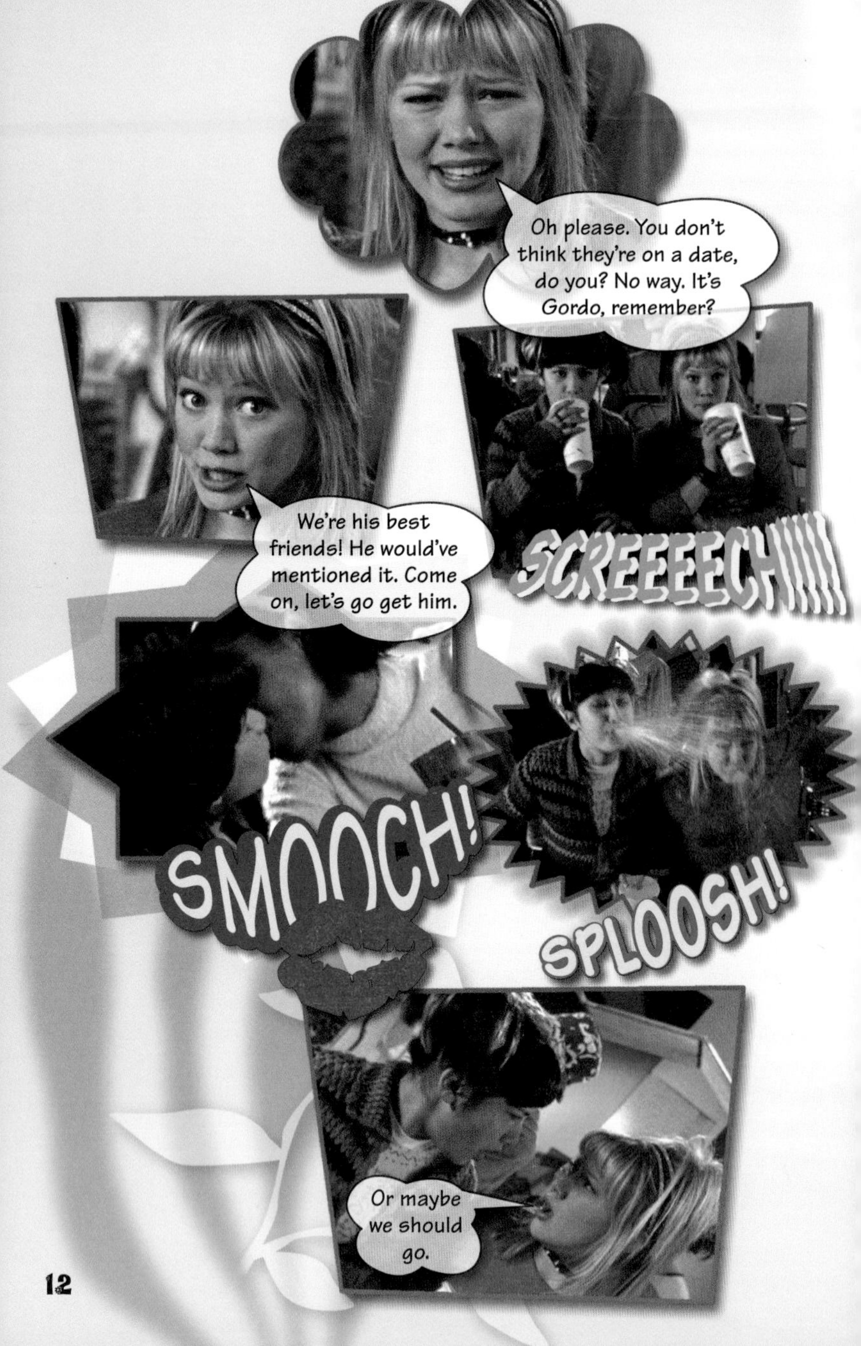
Oh please. You don't think they're on a date, do you? No way. It's Gordo, remember?
We're his best friends! He would've mentioned it. Come on, let's go get him.
SCREEEEECH!!!!!
SMOOCH!
SPLOOSH!
Or maybe we should go.

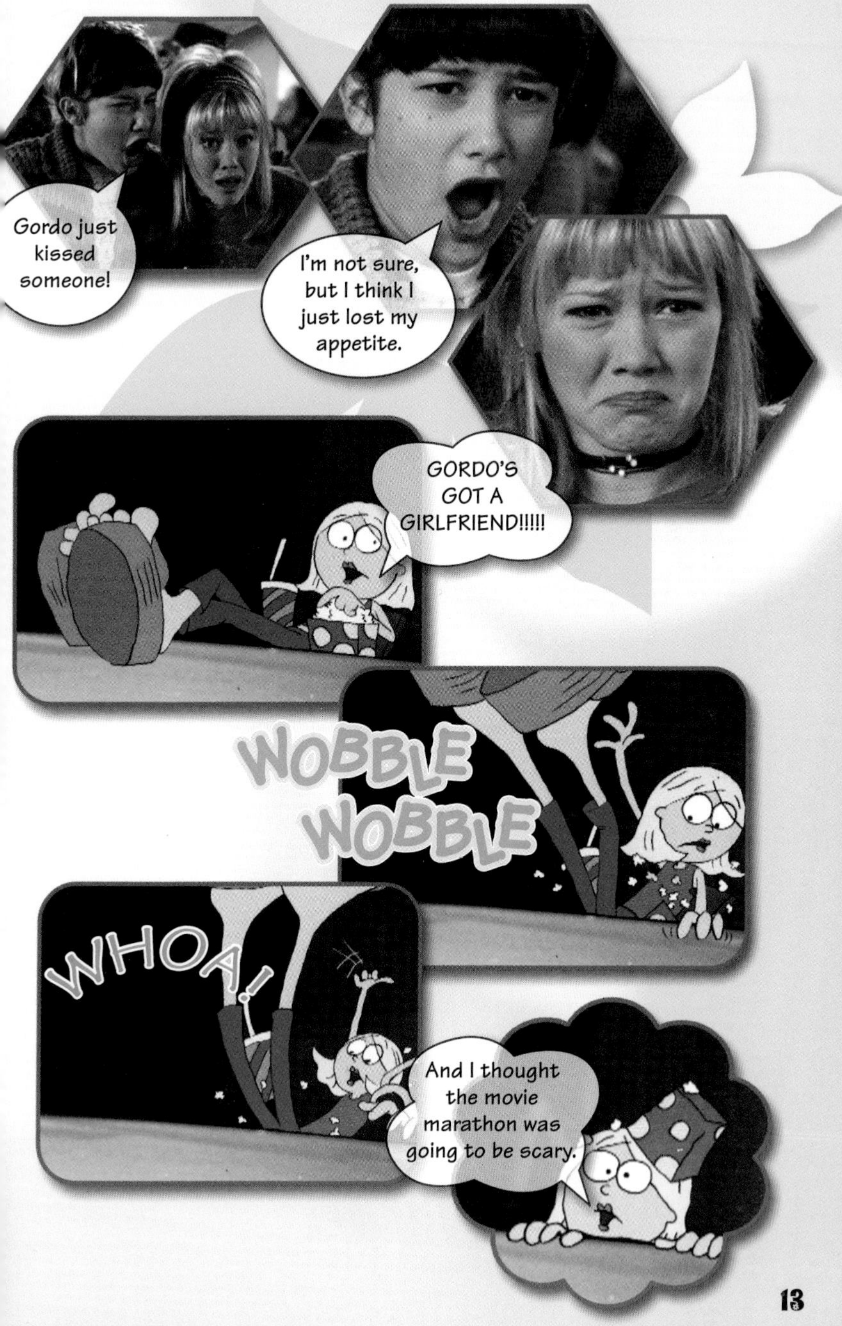

Gordo just kissed someone!
I'm not sure, but I think I just lost my appetite.
GORDO'S GOT A GIRLFRIEND!!!!!
WOBBLE WOBBLE
WHOA!
And I thought the movie marathon was going to be scary.

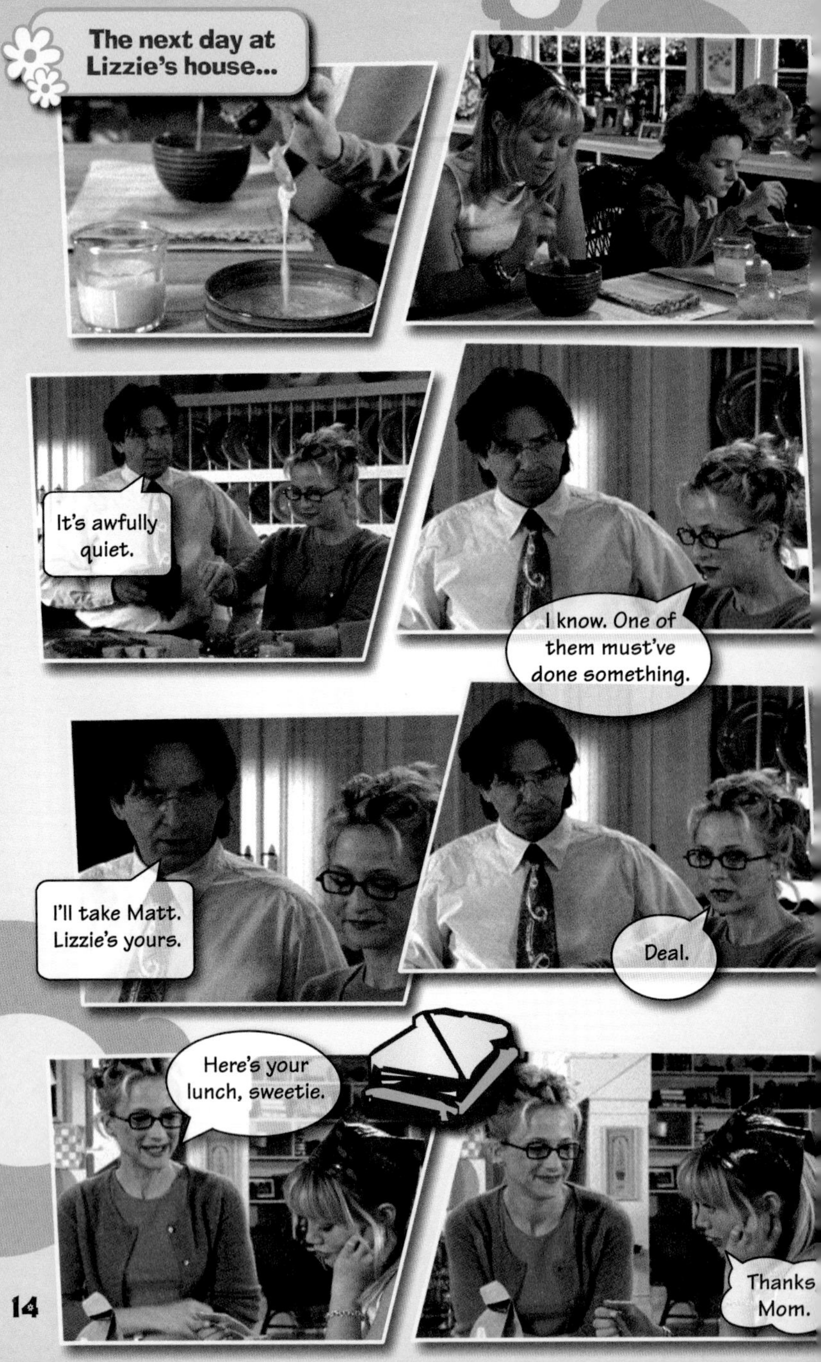
The next day at Lizzie's house...
It's awfully quiet.
I know. One of them must've done something.
I'll take Matt. Lizzie's yours.
Deal.
Here's your lunch, sweetie.
Thanks Mom.

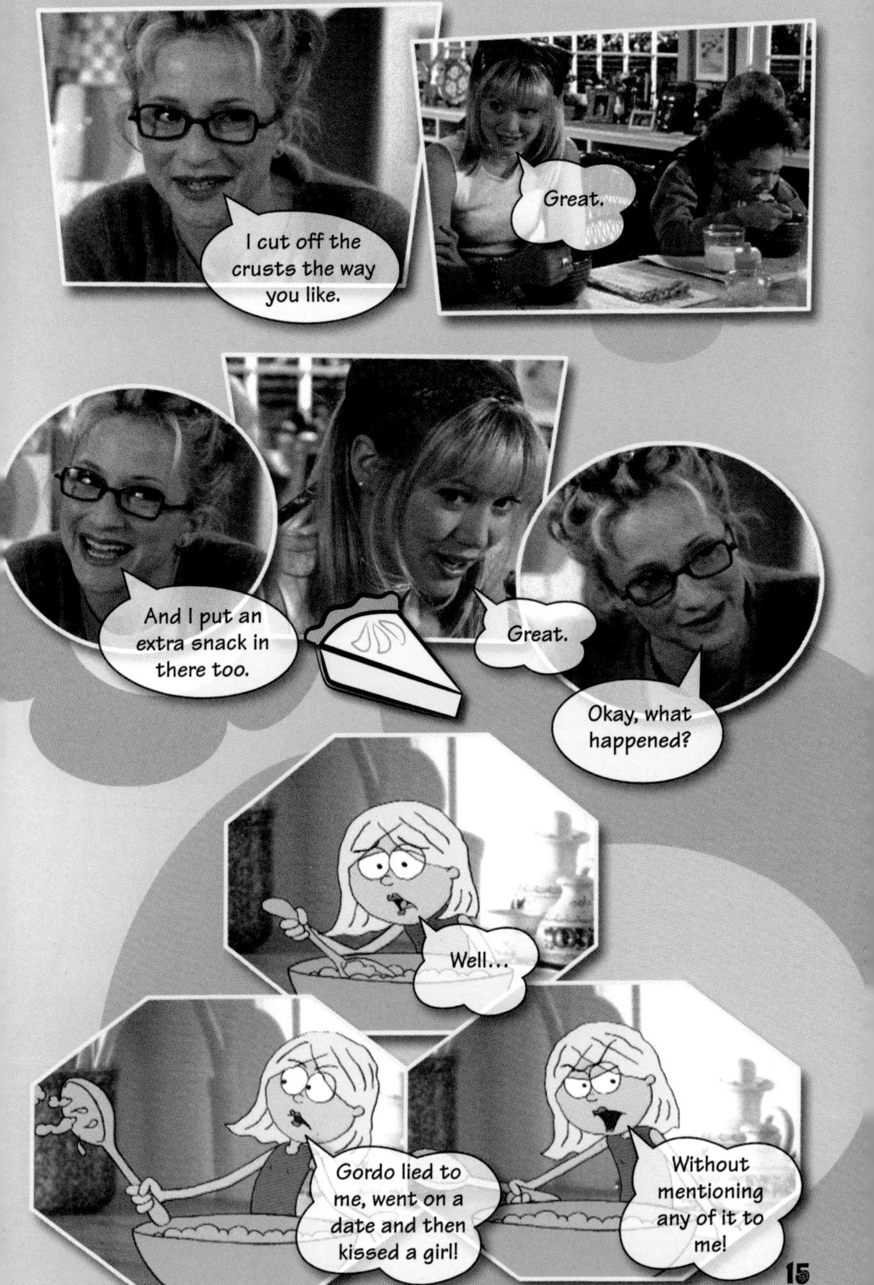
I cut off the crusts the way you like.
Great.
And I put an extra snack in there too.
Great.
Okay, what happened?
Well...
Gordo lied to me, went on a date and then kissed a girl!
Without mentioning any of it to me!

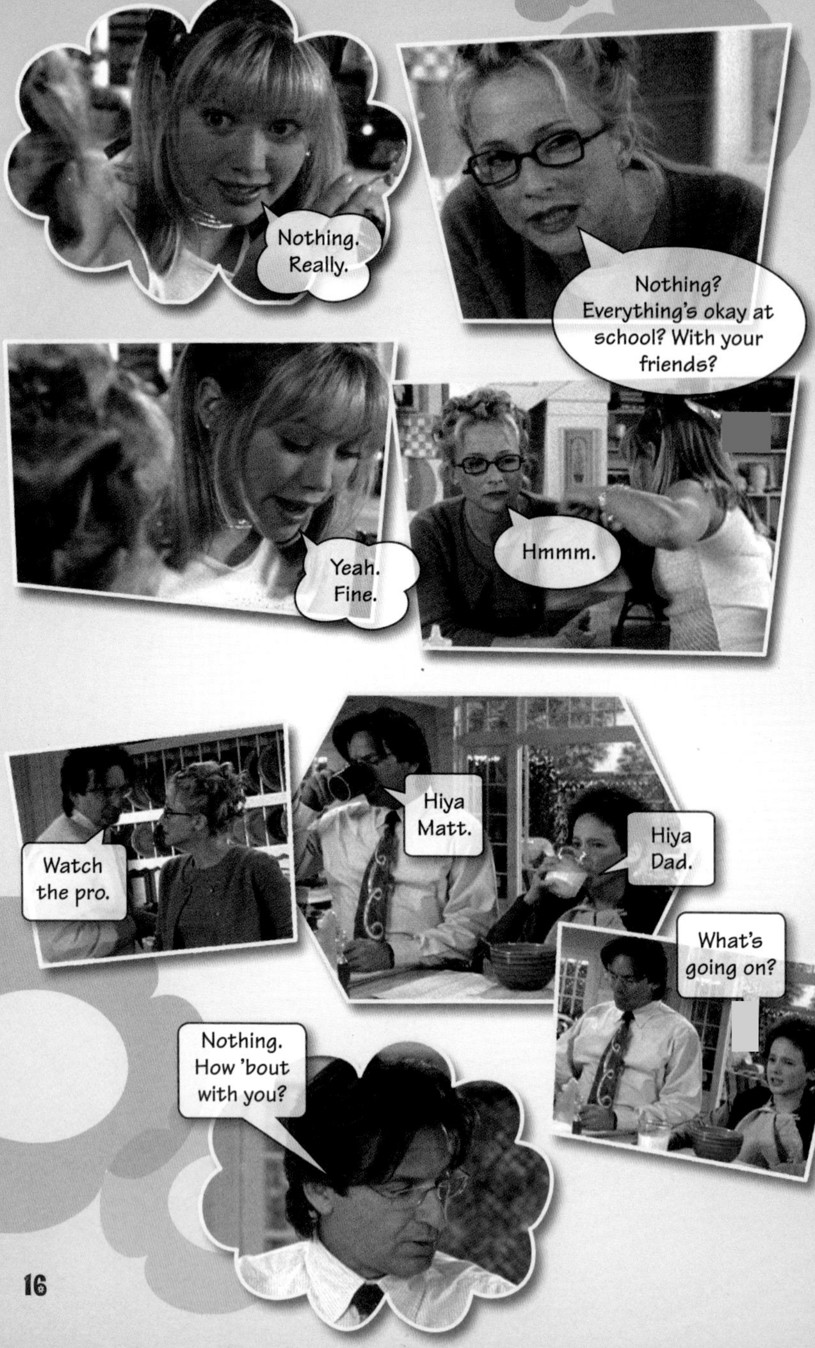

Nothing. Really.
Nothing? Everything's okay at school? With your friends?
Yeah. Fine.
Hmmm.
Watch the pro.
Hiya Matt.
Hiya Dad.
What's going on?
Nothing. How 'bout with you?

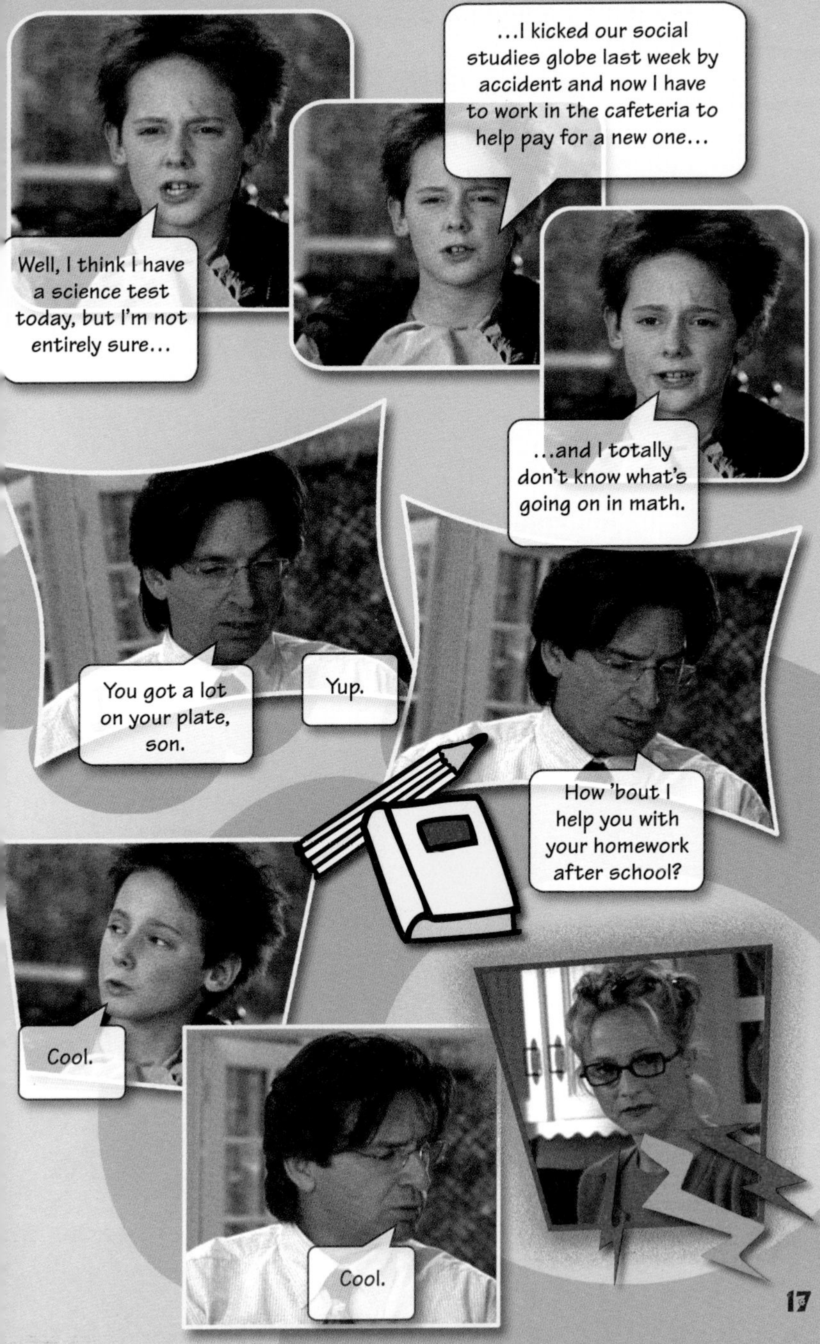
Well, I think I have a science test today, but I'm not entirely sure…
…I kicked our social studies globe last week by accident and now I have to work in the cafeteria to help pay for a new one…
…and I totally don't know what's going on in math.
You got a lot on your plate, son.
Yup.
How 'bout I help you with your homework after school?
Cool.
Cool.

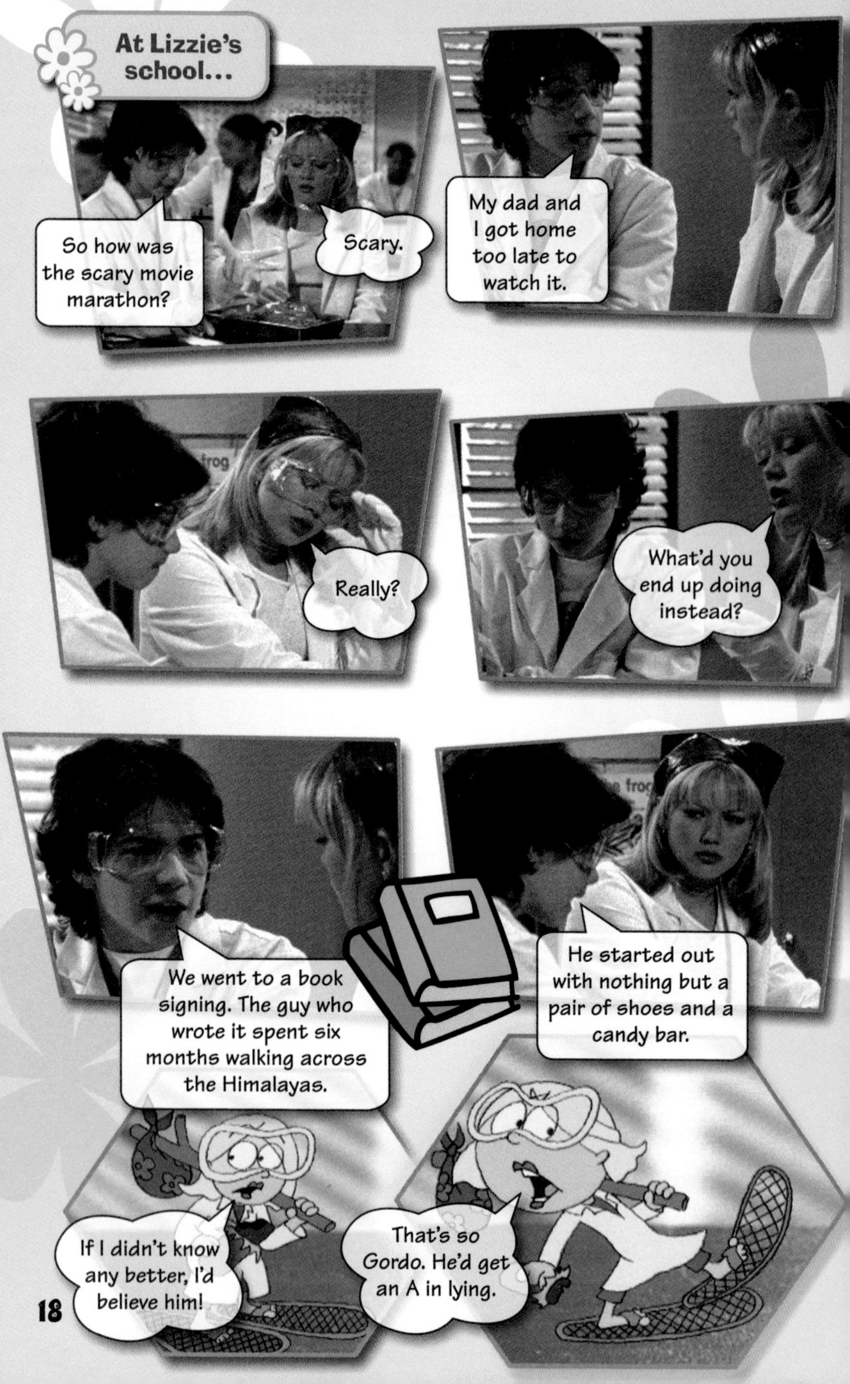
At Lizzie's school...
So how was the scary movie marathon?
Scary.
My dad and I got home too late to watch it.
Really?
What'd you end up doing instead?
We went to a book signing. The guy who wrote it spent six months walking across the Himalayas.
He started out with nothing but a pair of shoes and a candy bar.
If I didn't know any better, I'd believe him!
That's so Gordo. He'd get an A in lying.

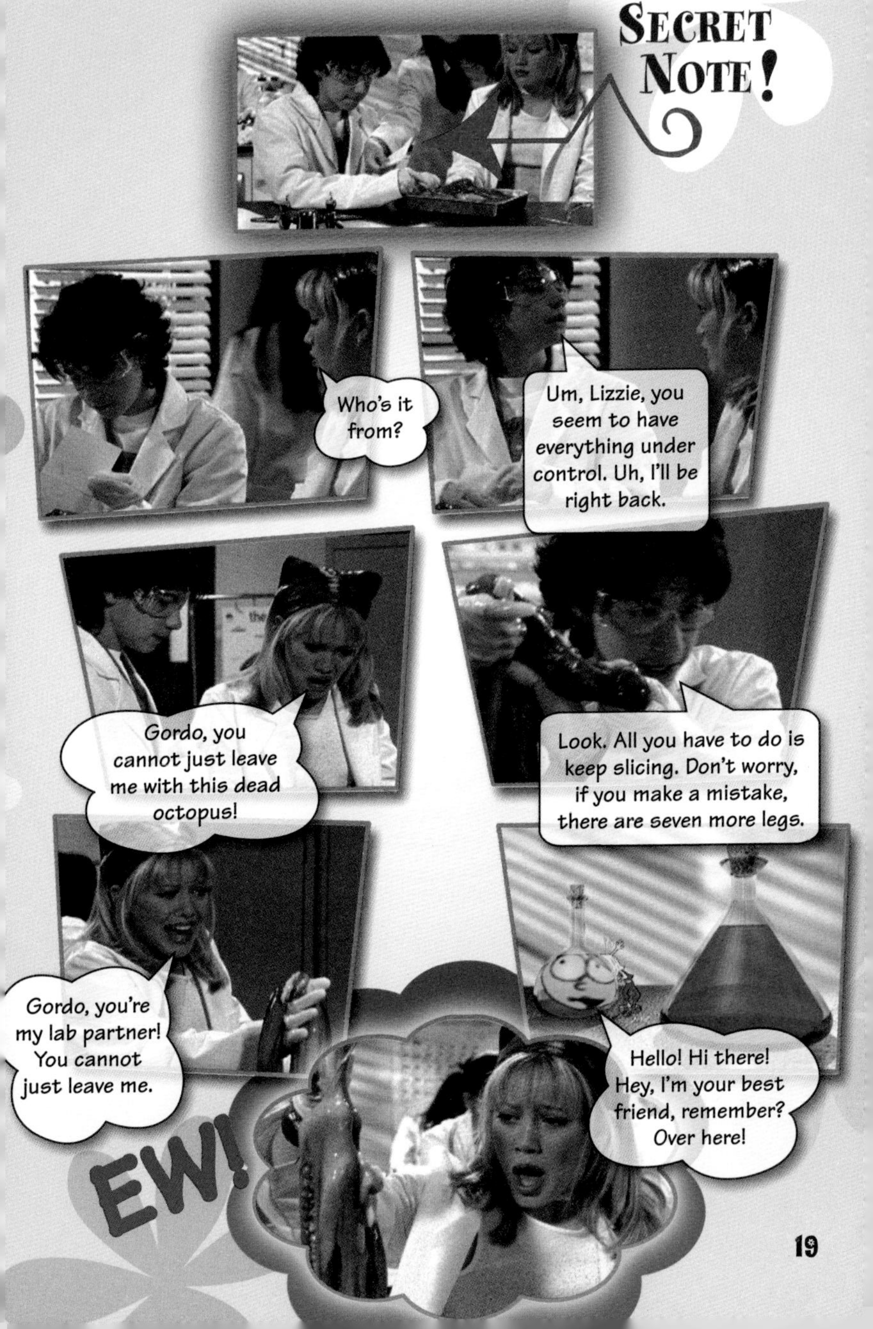
SECRET NOTE!
Who's it from?
Um, Lizzie, you seem to have everything under control. Uh, I'll be right back.
Gordo, you cannot just leave me with this dead octopus!
Look. All you have to do is keep slicing. Don't worry, if you make a mistake, there are seven more legs.
Gordo, you're my lab partner! You cannot just leave me.
Hello! Hi there! Hey, I'm your best friend, remember? Over here!
EW!

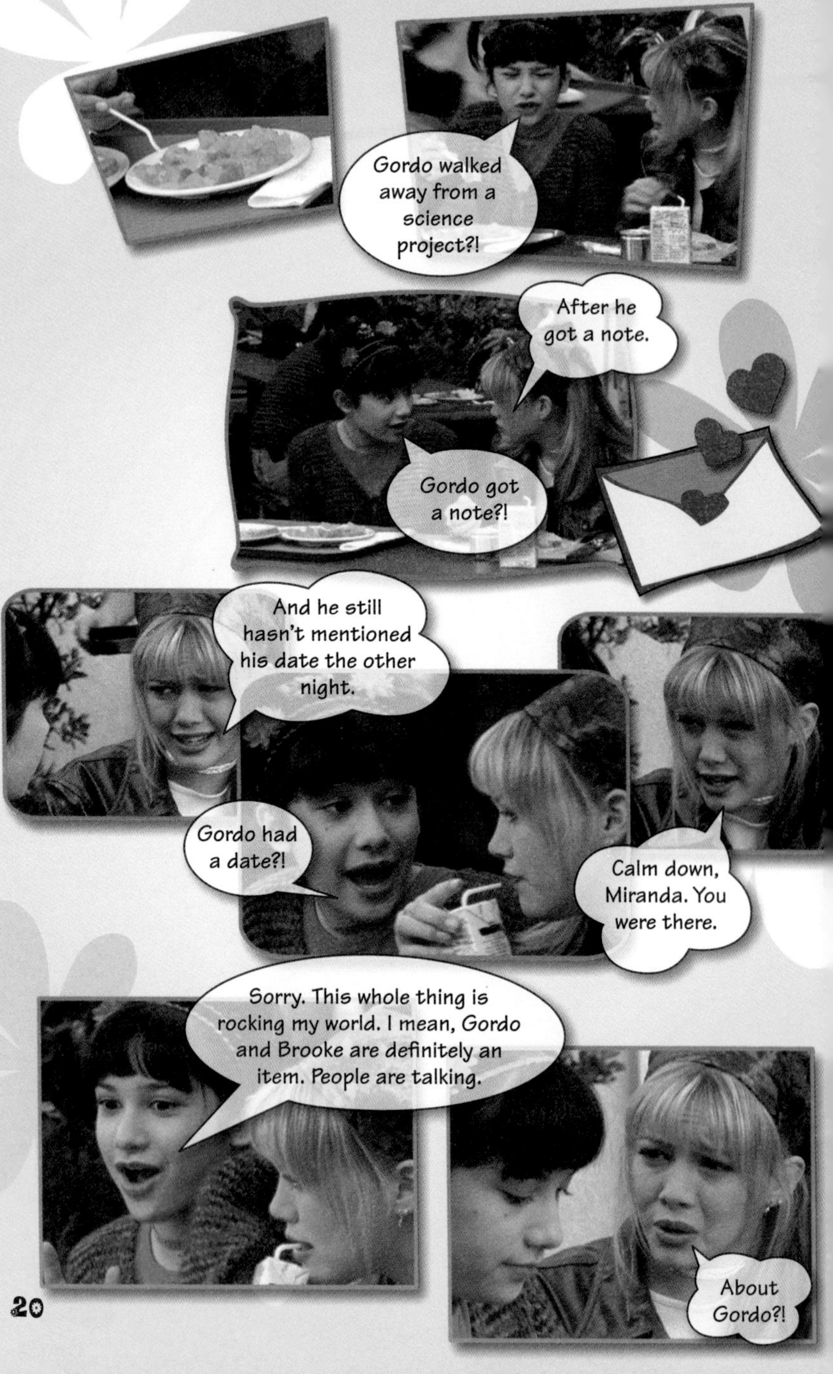
Gordo walked away from a science project?!
After he got a note.
Gordo got a note?!
And he still hasn't mentioned his date the other night.
Gordo had a date?!
Calm down, Miranda. You were there.
Sorry. This whole thing is rocking my world. I mean, Gordo and Brooke are definitely an item. People are talking.
About Gordo?!

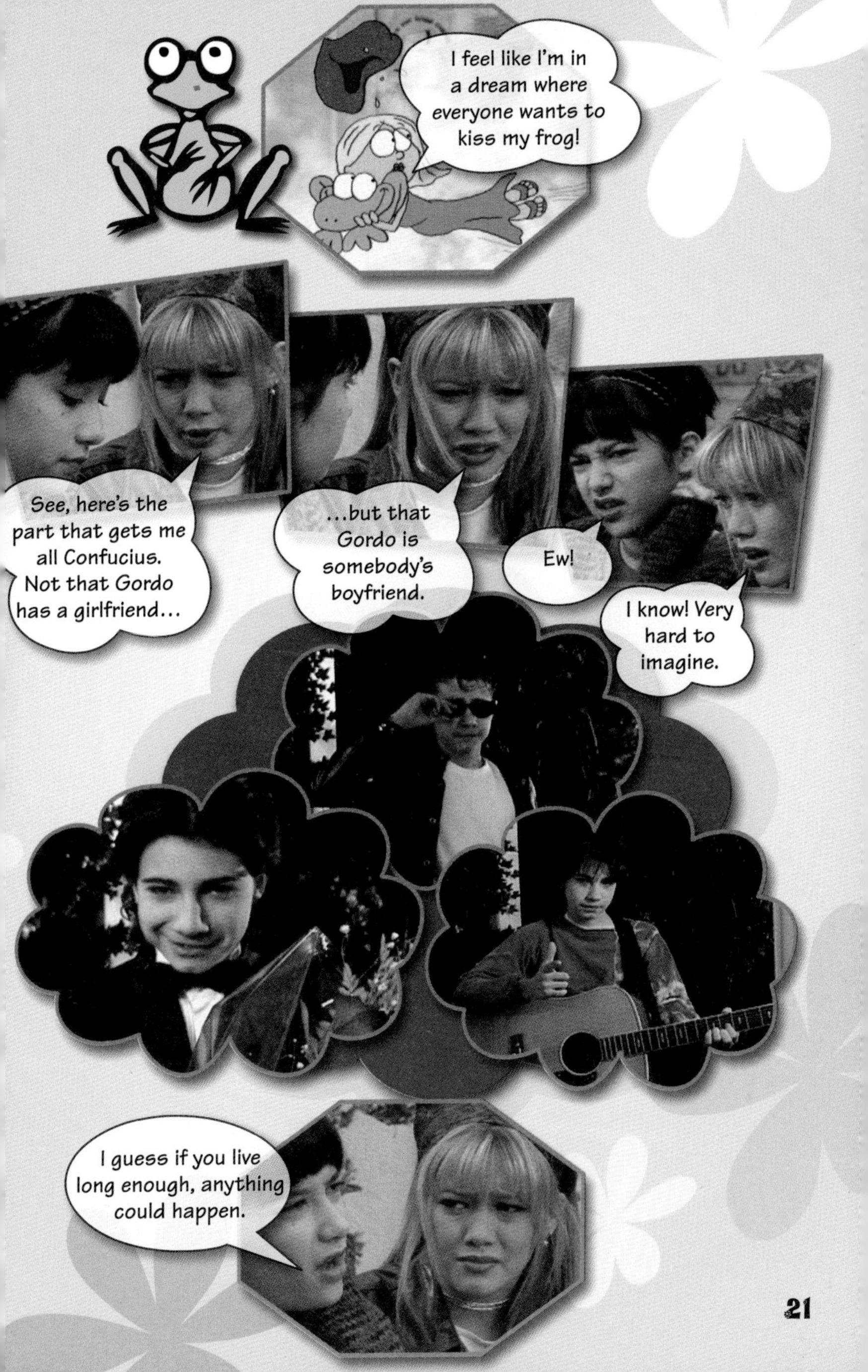
I feel like I'm in a dream where everyone wants to kiss my frog!
See, here's the part that gets me all Confucius. Not that Gordo has a girlfriend...
...but that Gordo is somebody's boyfriend.
Ew!
I know! Very hard to imagine.
I guess if you live long enough, anything could happen.

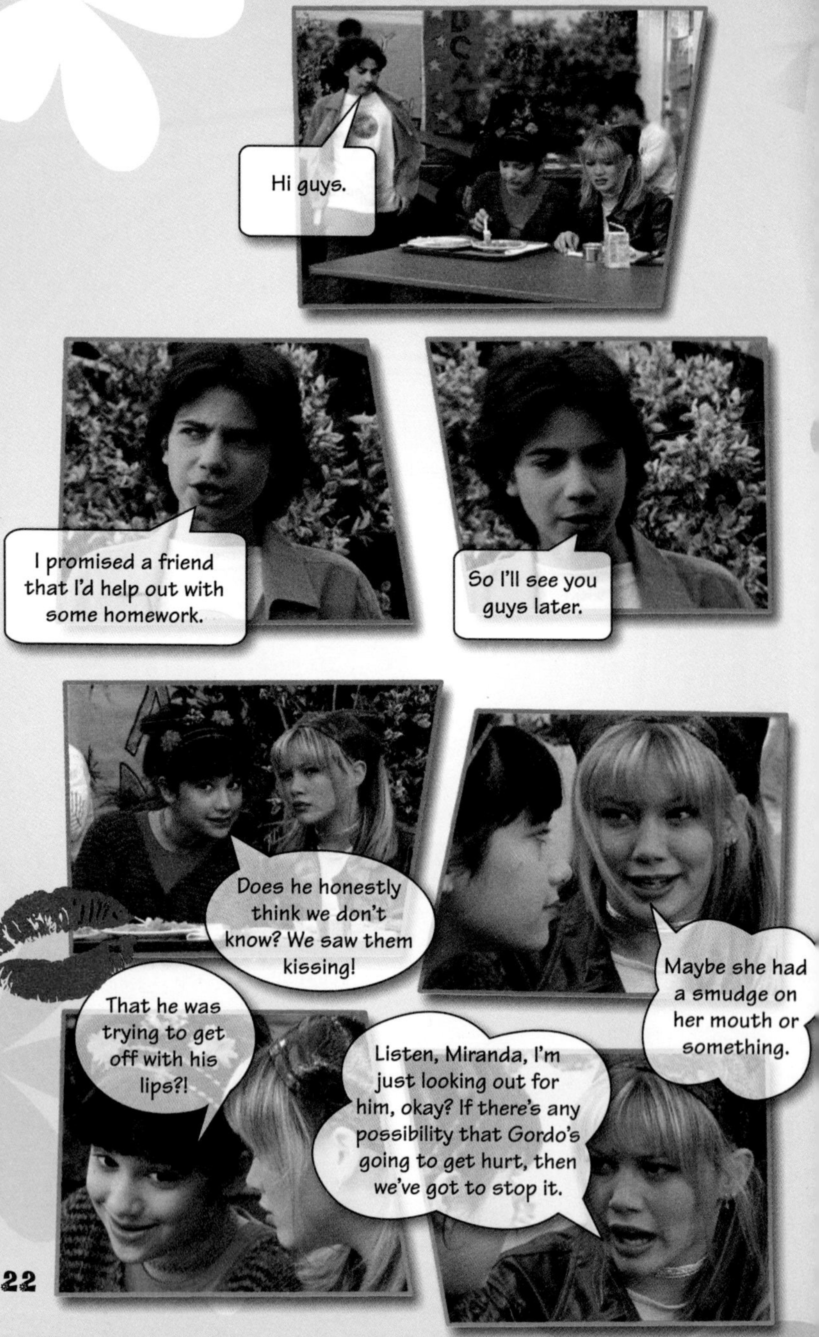
Hi guys.
I promised a friend that I'd help out with some homework.
So I'll see you guys later.
Does he honestly think we don't know? We saw them kissing!
Maybe she had a smudge on her mouth or something.
That he was trying to get off with his lips?!
Listen, Miranda, I'm just looking out for him, okay? If there's any possibility that Gordo's going to get hurt, then we've got to stop it.

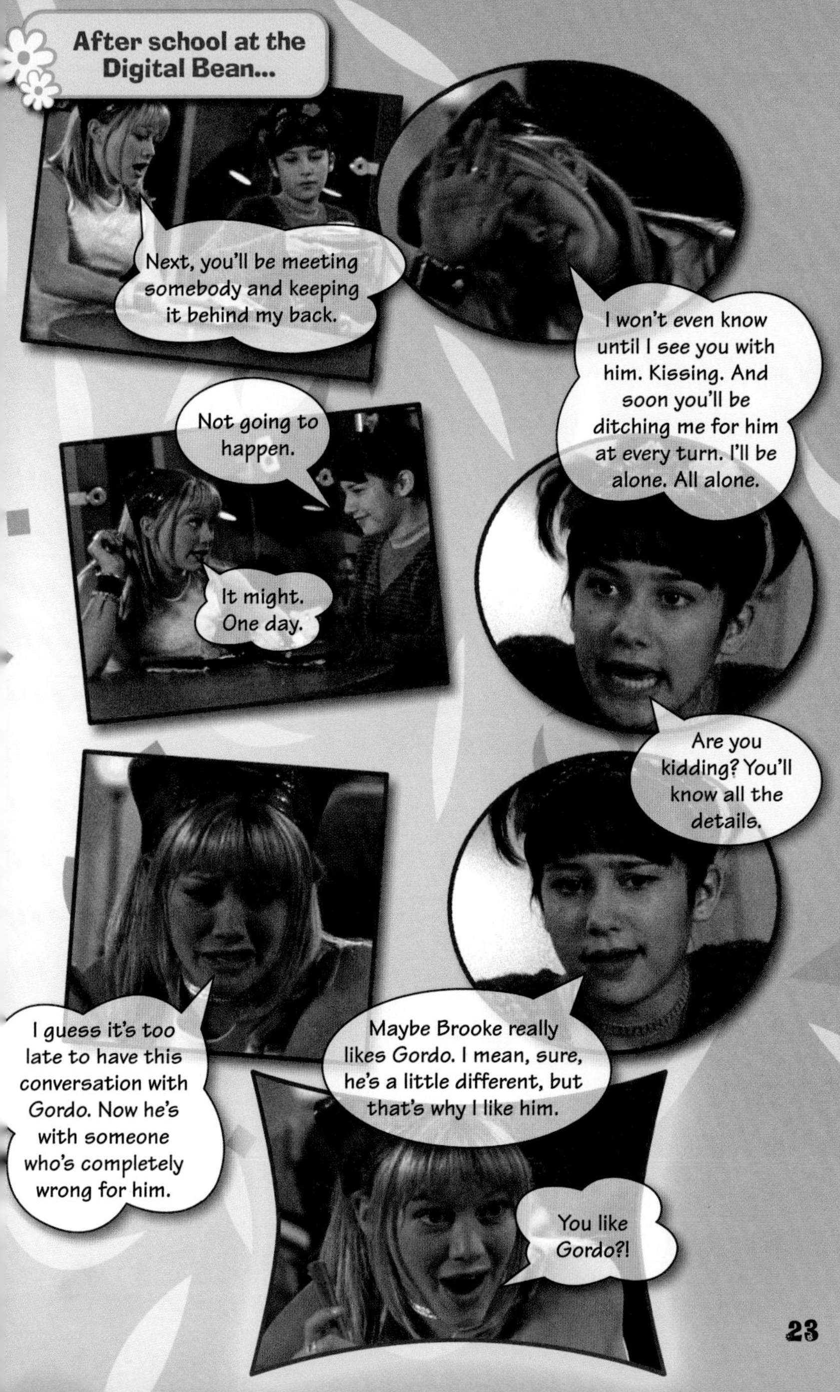
After school at the Digital Bean...
Next, you'll be meeting somebody and keeping it behind my back.
I won't even know until I see you with him. Kissing. And soon you'll be ditching me for him at every turn. I'll be alone. All alone.
Not going to happen.
It might. One day.
Are you kidding? You'll know all the details.
I guess it's too late to have this conversation with Gordo. Now he's with someone who's completely wrong for him.
Maybe Brooke really likes Gordo. I mean, sure, he's a little different, but that's why I like him.
You like Gordo?!

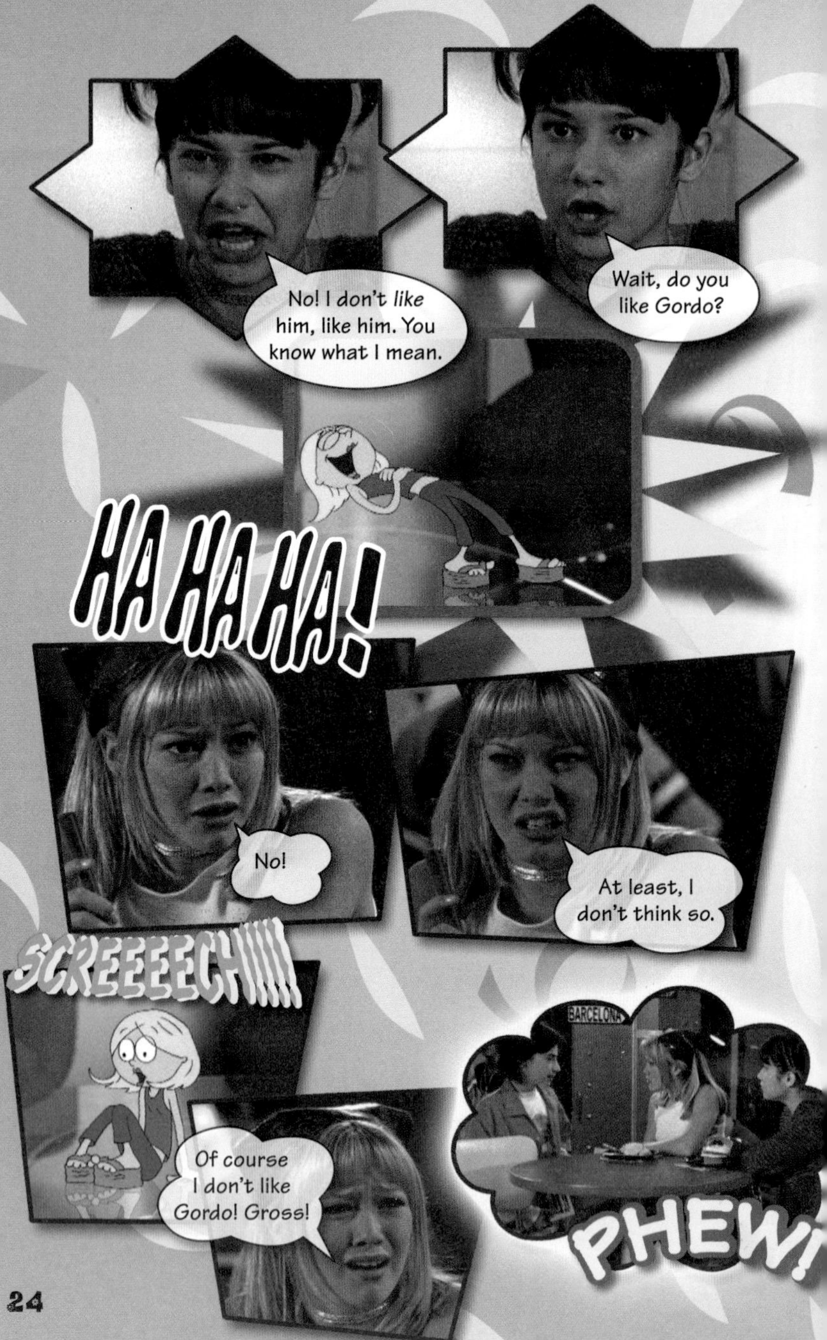
No! I don't like him, like him. You know what I mean.
Wait, do you like Gordo?
HA HA HA HA!
No!
At least, I don't think so.
SCREEEEECH!!!!
BARCELONA
Of course I don't like Gordo! Gross!
PHEW!

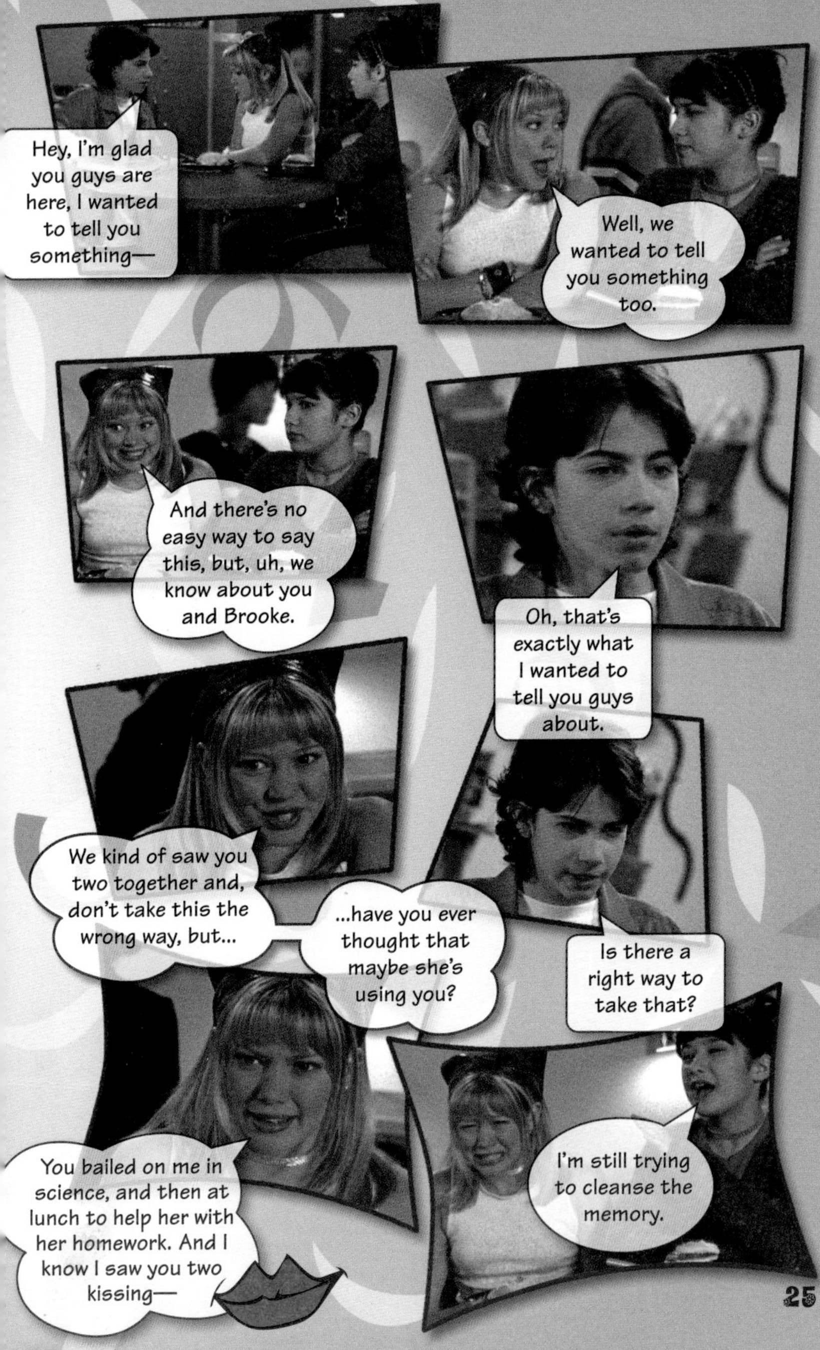
Hey, I'm glad you guys are here, I wanted to tell you something—
Well, we wanted to tell you something too.
And there's no easy way to say this, but, uh, we know about you and Brooke.
Oh, that's exactly what I wanted to tell you guys about.
We kind of saw you two together and, don't take this the wrong way, but...
...have you ever thought that maybe she's using you?
Is there a right way to take that?
You bailed on me in science, and then at lunch to help her with her homework. And I know I saw you two kissing—
I'm still trying to cleanse the memory.

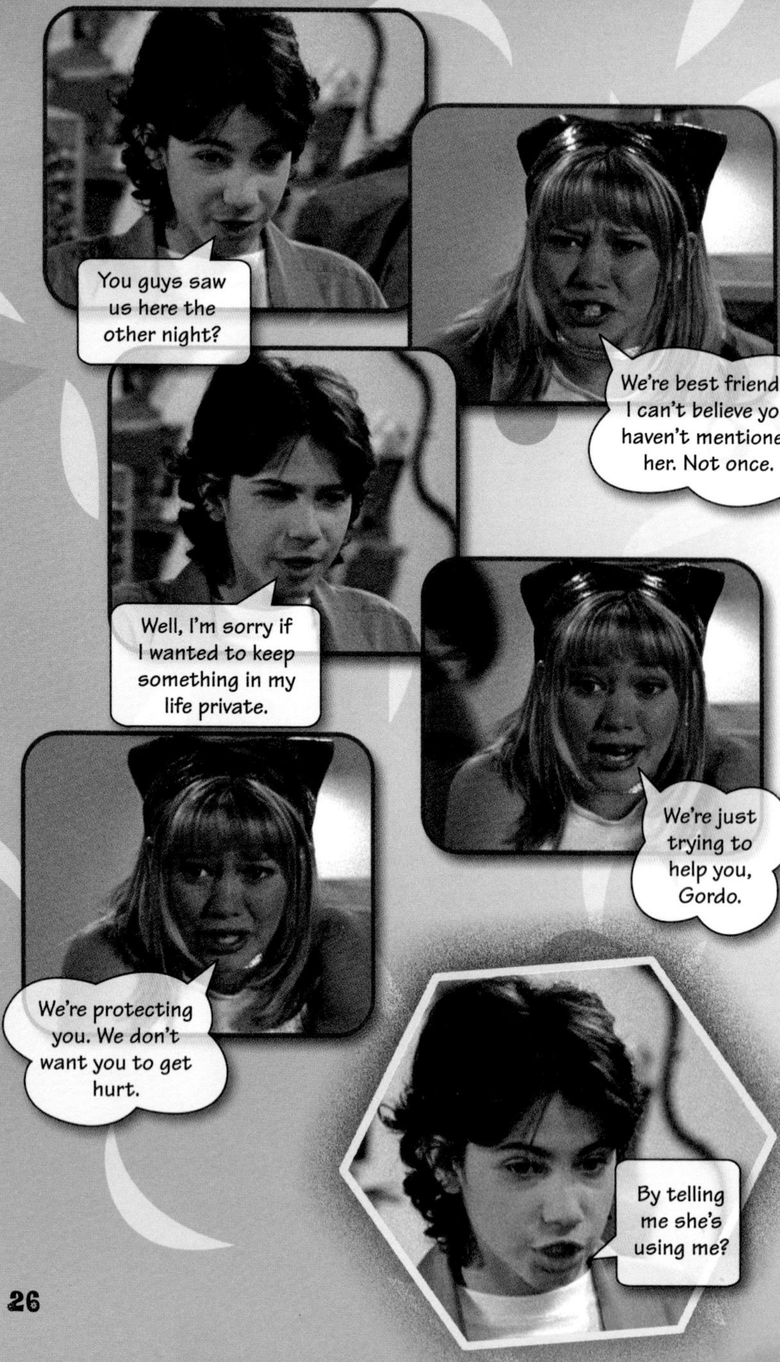
You guys saw us here the other night?
We're best friends. I can't believe you haven't mentioned her. Not once.
Well, I'm sorry if I wanted to keep something in my life private.
We're just trying to help you, Gordo.
We're protecting you. We don't want you to get hurt.
By telling me she's using me?

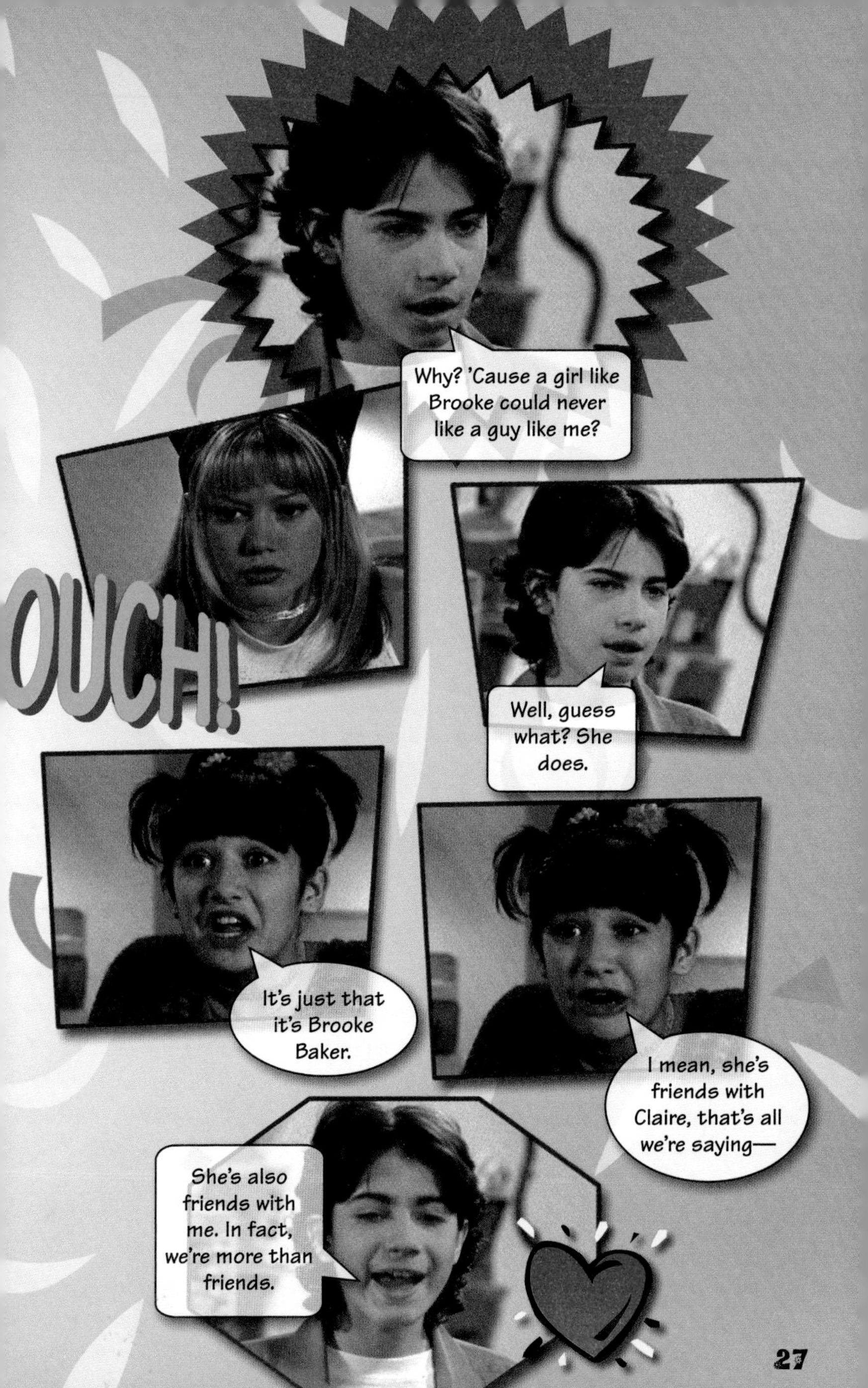
Why? 'Cause a girl like Brooke could never like a guy like me?
OUCH!
Well, guess what? She does.
It's just that it's Brooke Baker.
I mean, she's friends with Claire, that's all we're saying—
She's also friends with me. In fact, we're more than friends.

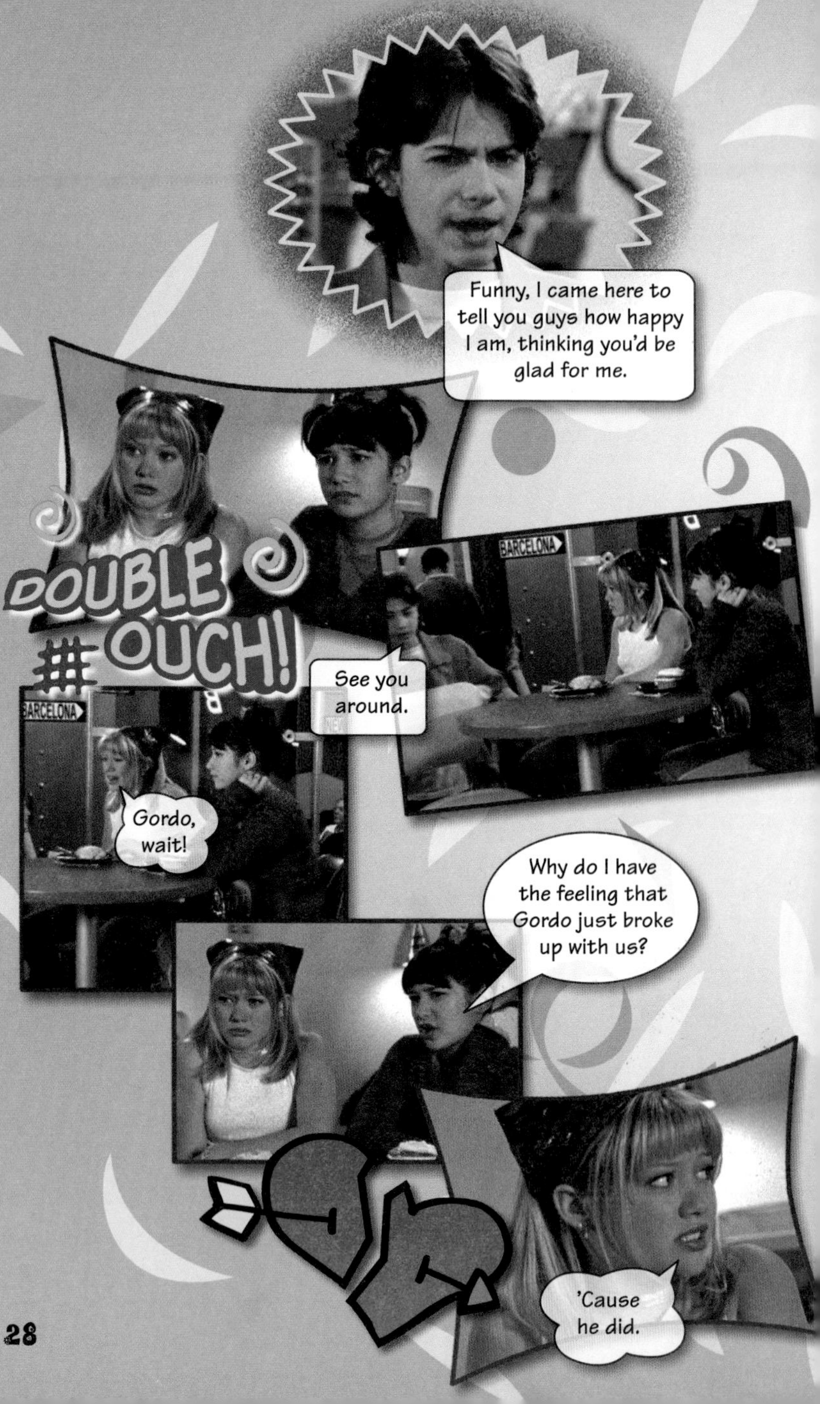
Funny, I came here to tell you guys how happy I am, thinking you'd be glad for me.
DOUBLE OUCH!
BARCELONA
See you around.
BARCELONA
Gordo, wait!
Why do I have the feeling that Gordo just broke up with us?
'Cause he did.

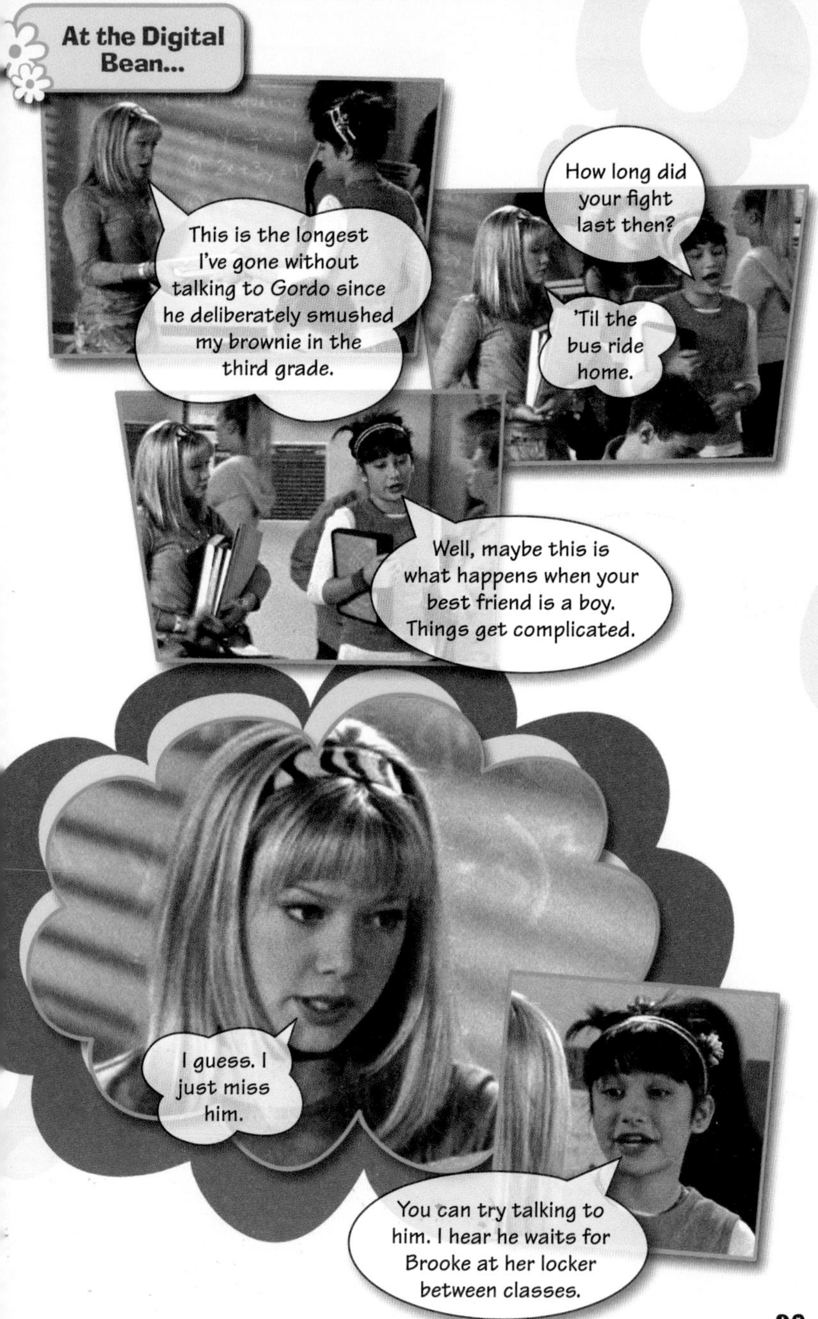
At the Digital Bean...
This is the longest I've gone without talking to Gordo since he deliberately smushed my brownie in the third grade.
How long did your fight last then?
'Til the bus ride home.
Well, maybe this is what happens when your best friend is a boy. Things get complicated.
I guess. I just miss him.
You can try talking to him. I hear he waits for Brooke at her locker between classes.

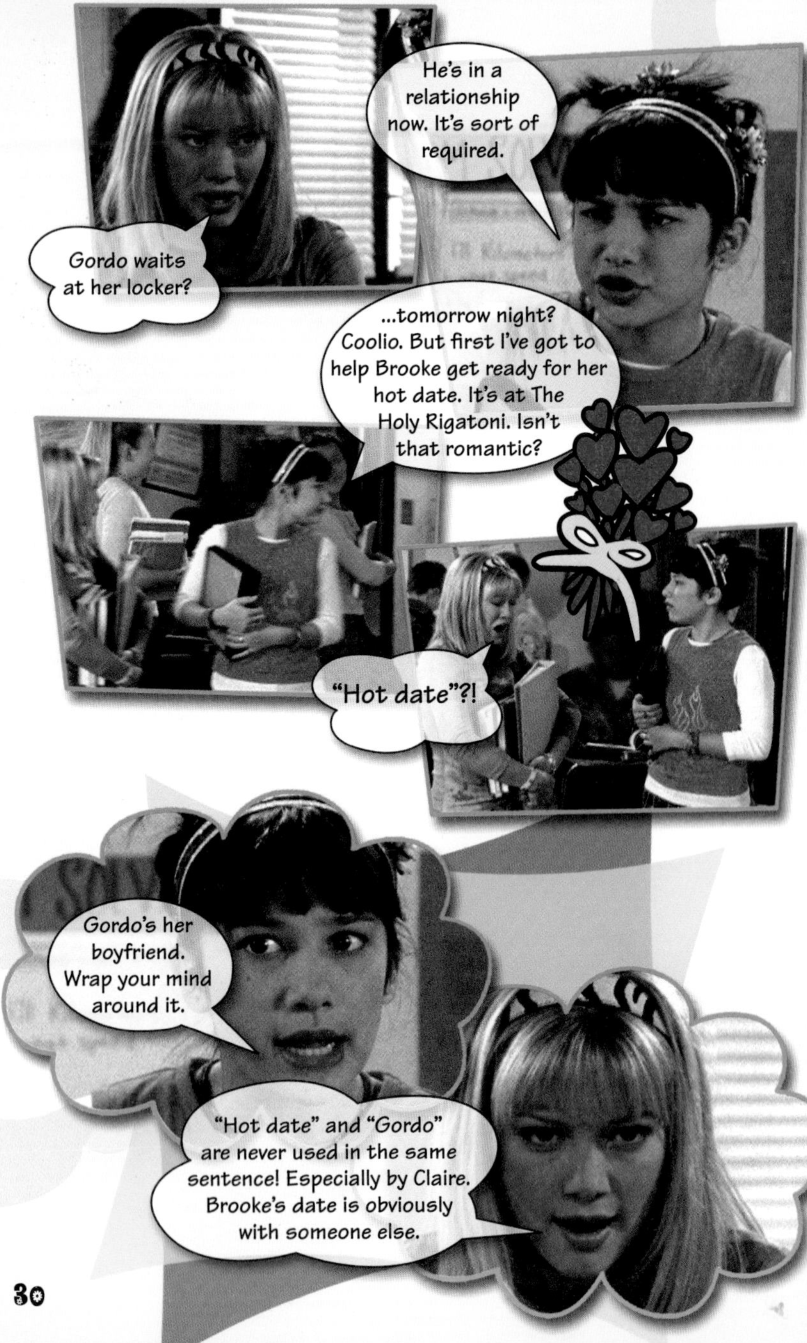

Gordo waits at her locker?
He's in a relationship now. It's sort of required.
...tomorrow night? Coolio. But first I've got to help Brooke get ready for her hot date. It's at The Holy Rigatoni. Isn't that romantic?
"Hot date"?!
Gordo's her boyfriend. Wrap your mind around it.
"Hot date" and "Gordo" are never used in the same sentence! Especially by Claire. Brooke's date is obviously with someone else.

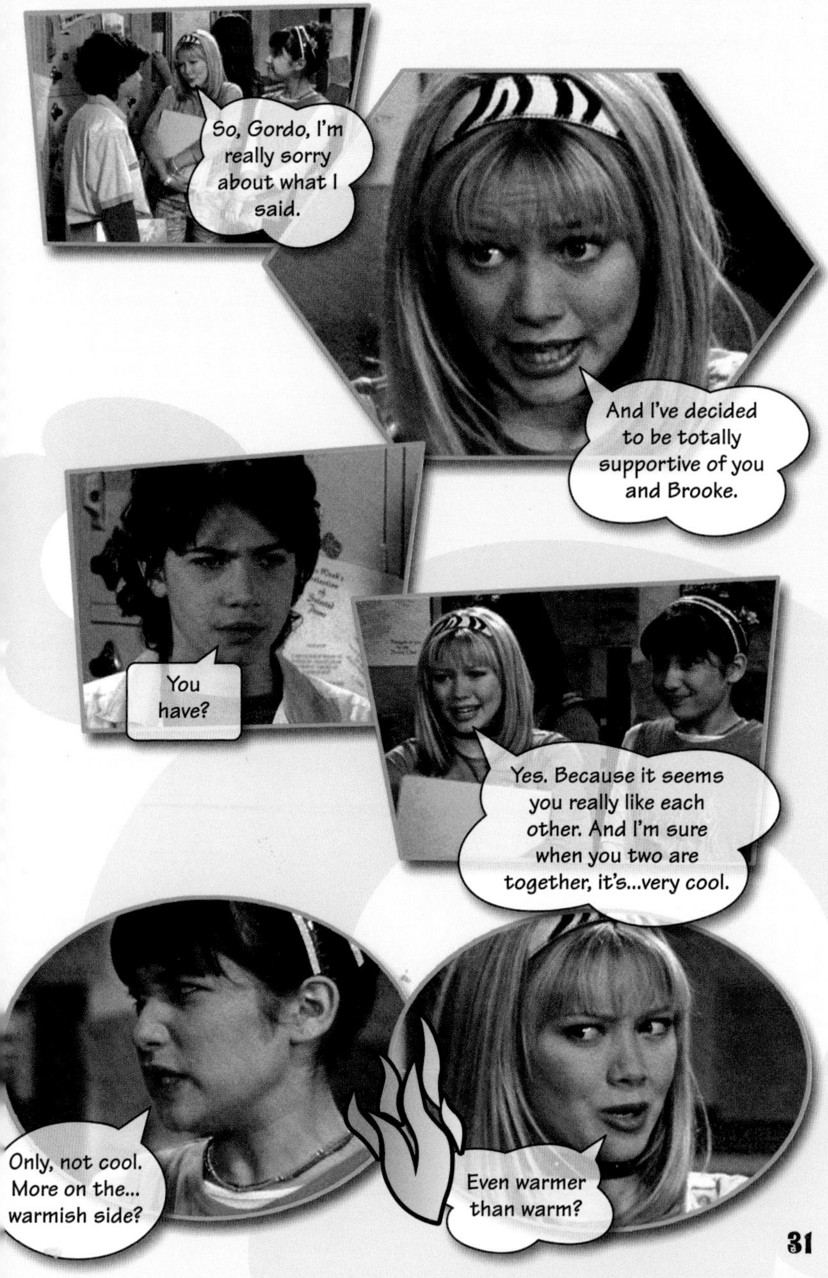
So, Gordo, I'm really sorry about what I said.
And I've decided to be totally supportive of you and Brooke.
You have?
Yes. Because it seems you really like each other. And I'm sure when you two are together, it's...very cool.
Only, not cool. More on the... warmish side?
Even warmer than warm?

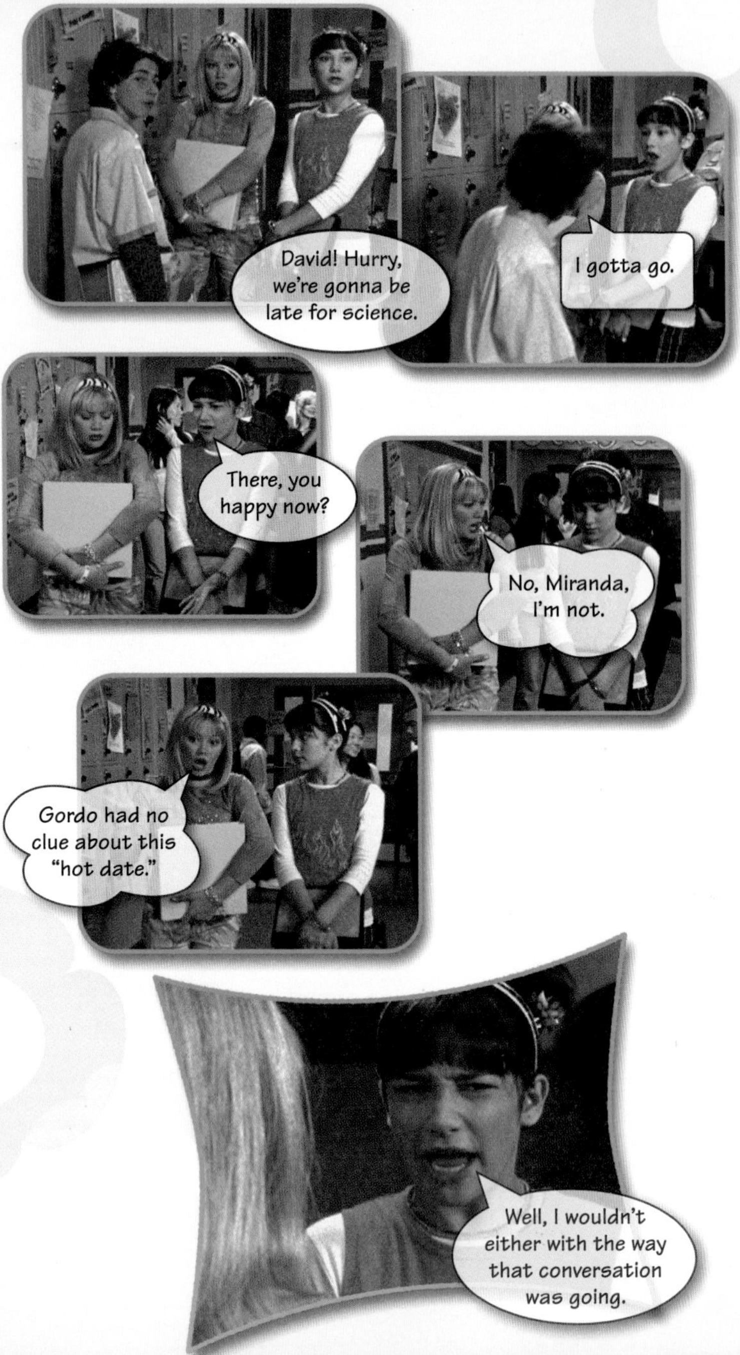
David! Hurry, we're gonna be late for science.
I gotta go.
There, you happy now?
No, Miranda, I'm not.
Gordo had no clue about this "hot date."
Well, I wouldn't either with the way that conversation was going.

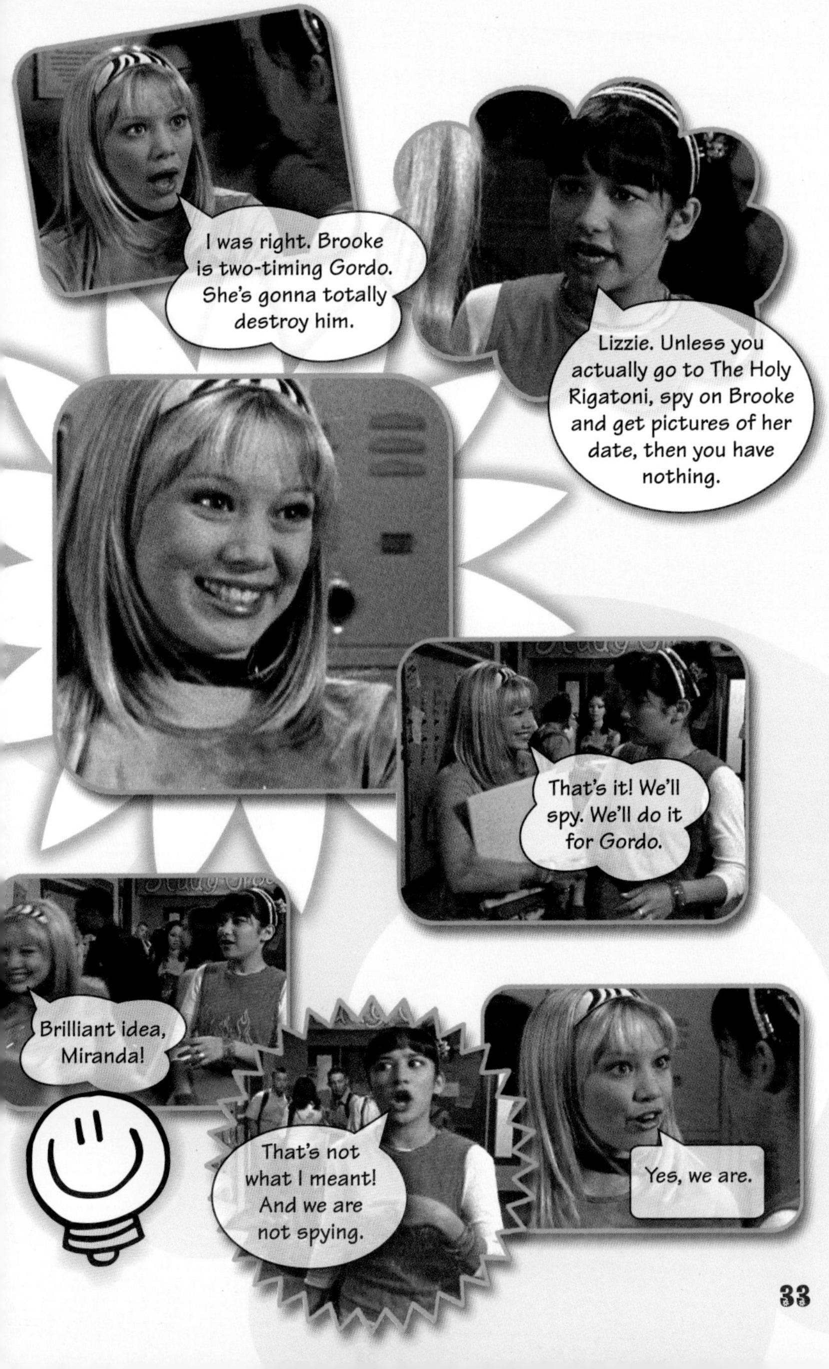

I was right. Brooke is two-timing Gordo. She's gonna totally destroy him.
Lizzie. Unless you actually go to The Holy Rigatoni, spy on Brooke and get pictures of her date, then you have nothing.
That's it! We'll spy. We'll do it for Gordo.
Brilliant idea, Miranda!
That's not what I meant! And we are not spying.
Yes, we are.

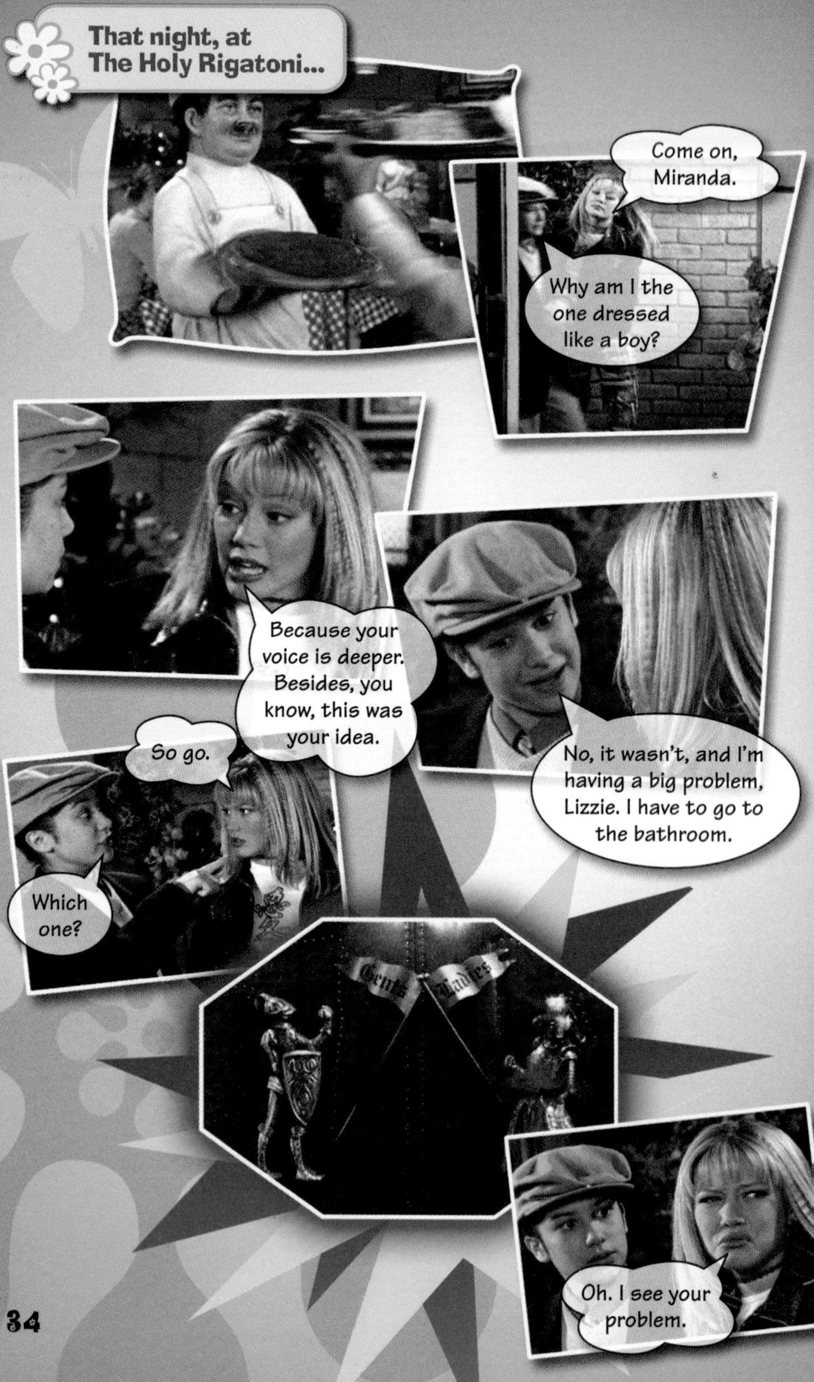
That night, at The Holy Rigatoni...
Come on, Miranda.
Why am I the one dressed like a boy?
Because your voice is deeper. Besides, you know, this was your idea.
No, it wasn't, and I'm having a big problem, Lizzie. I have to go to the bathroom.
So go.
Which one?
Gents
Ladies
Oh. I see your problem.

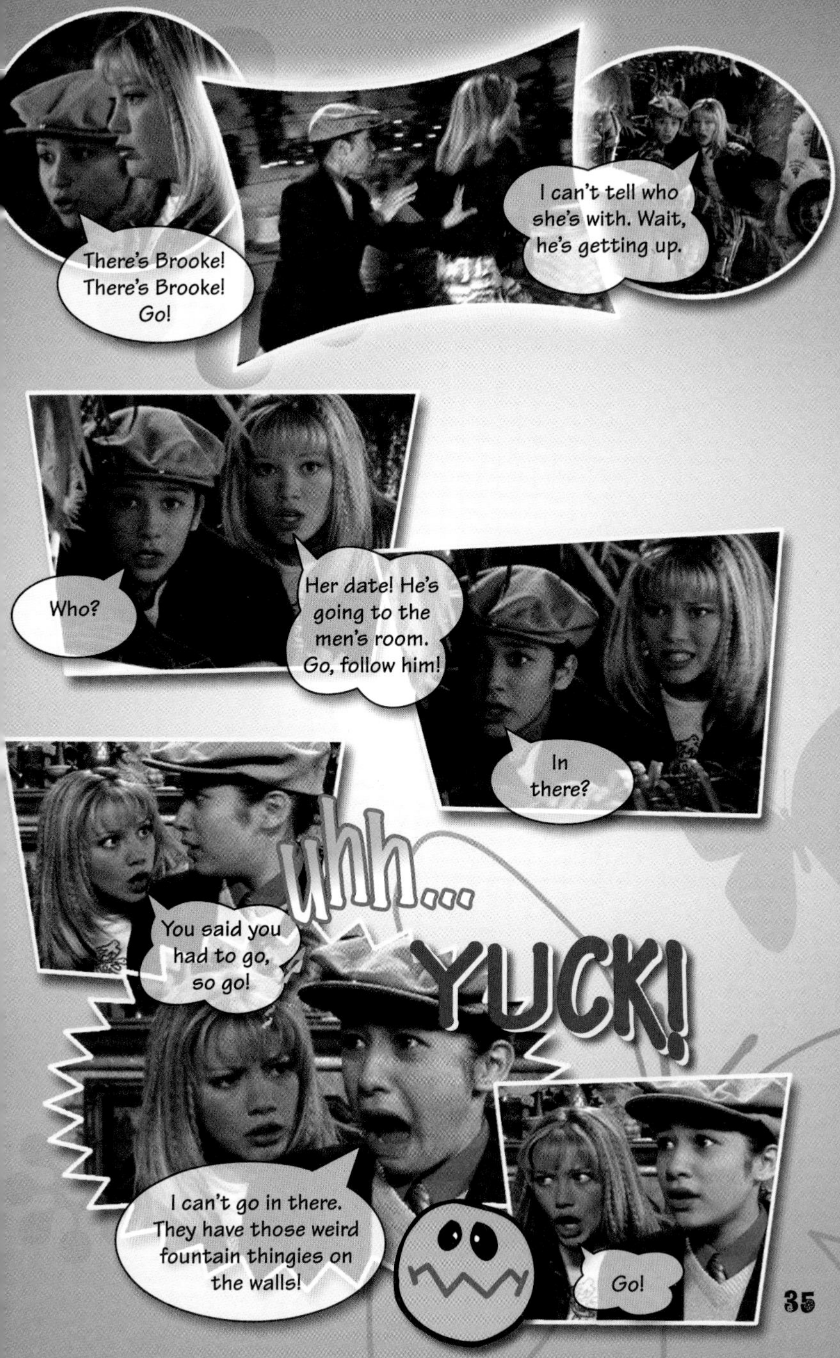
There's Brooke! There's Brooke! Go!
I can't tell who she's with. Wait, he's getting up.
Who?
Her date! He's going to the men's room. Go, follow him!
In there?
uhh...
You said you had to go, so go!
YUCK!
I can't go in there. They have those weird fountain thingies on the walls!
Go!

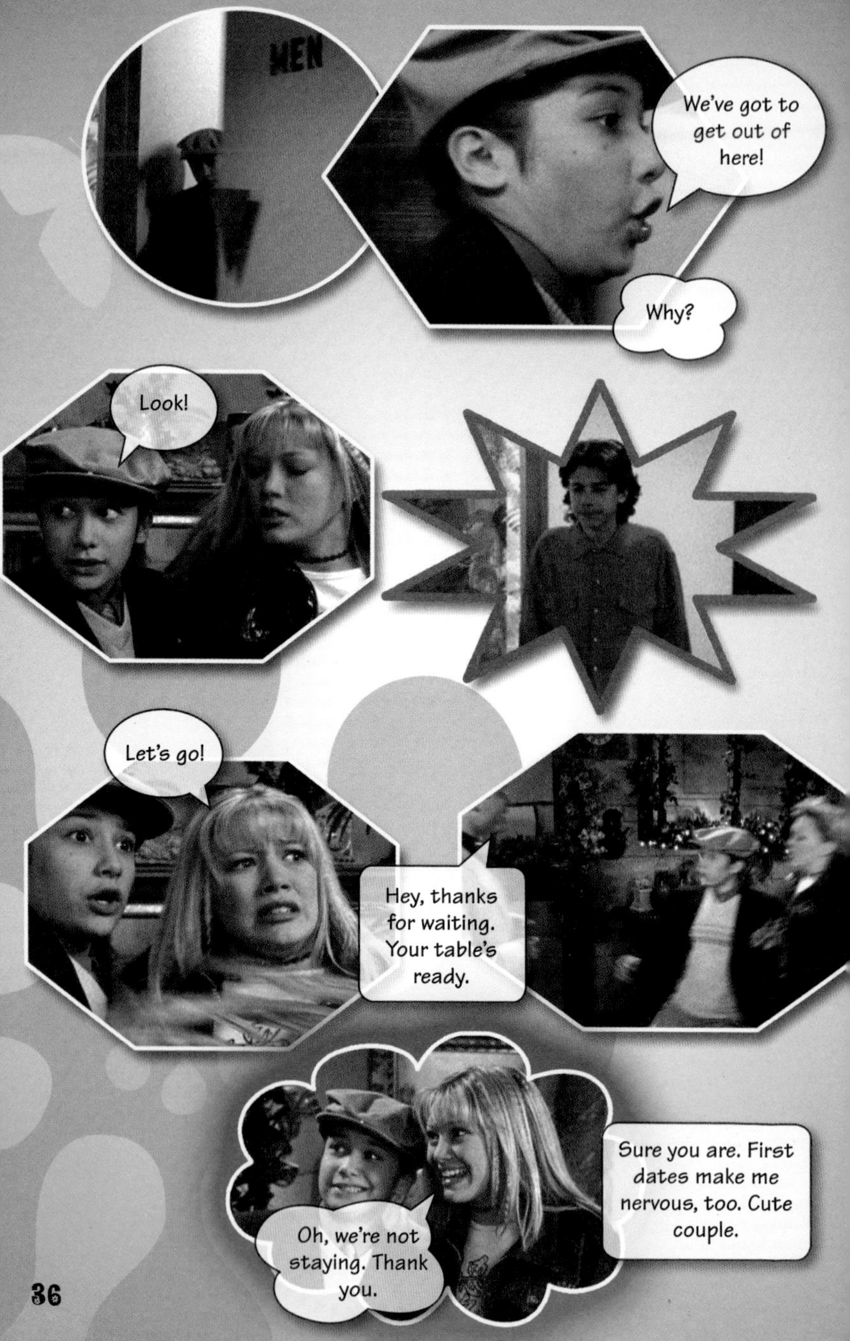

MEN
We've got to get out of here!
Why?
Look!
Let's go!
Hey, thanks for waiting. Your table's ready.
Sure you are. First dates make me nervous, too. Cute couple.
Oh, we're not staying. Thank you.

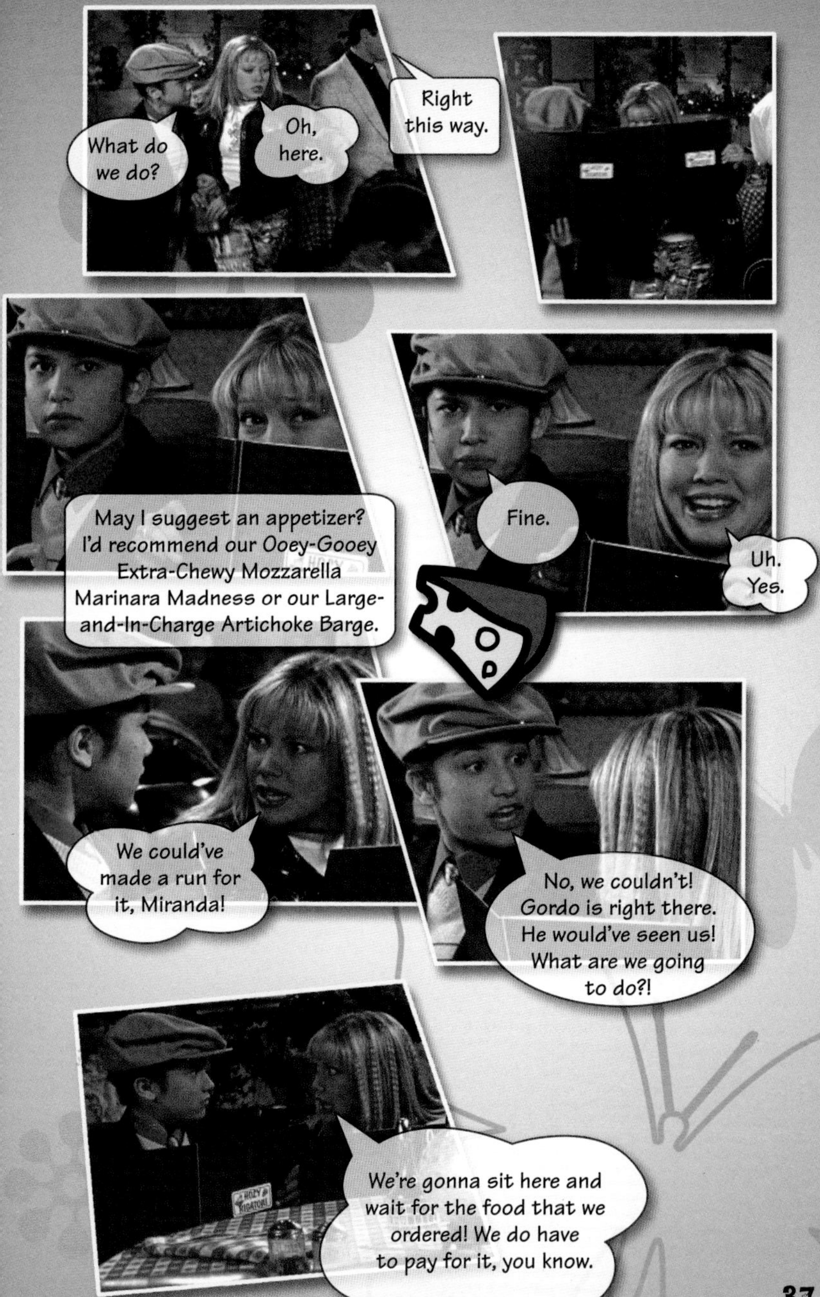
What do we do?
Oh, here.
Right this way.
May I suggest an appetizer? I'd recommend our Ooey-Gooey Extra-Chewy Mozzarella Marinara Madness or our Large-and-In-Charge Artichoke Barge.
Fine.
Uh. Yes.
We could've made a run for it, Miranda!
No, we couldn't! Gordo is right there. He would've seen us! What are we going to do?!
We're gonna sit here and wait for the food that we ordered! We do have to pay for it, you know.

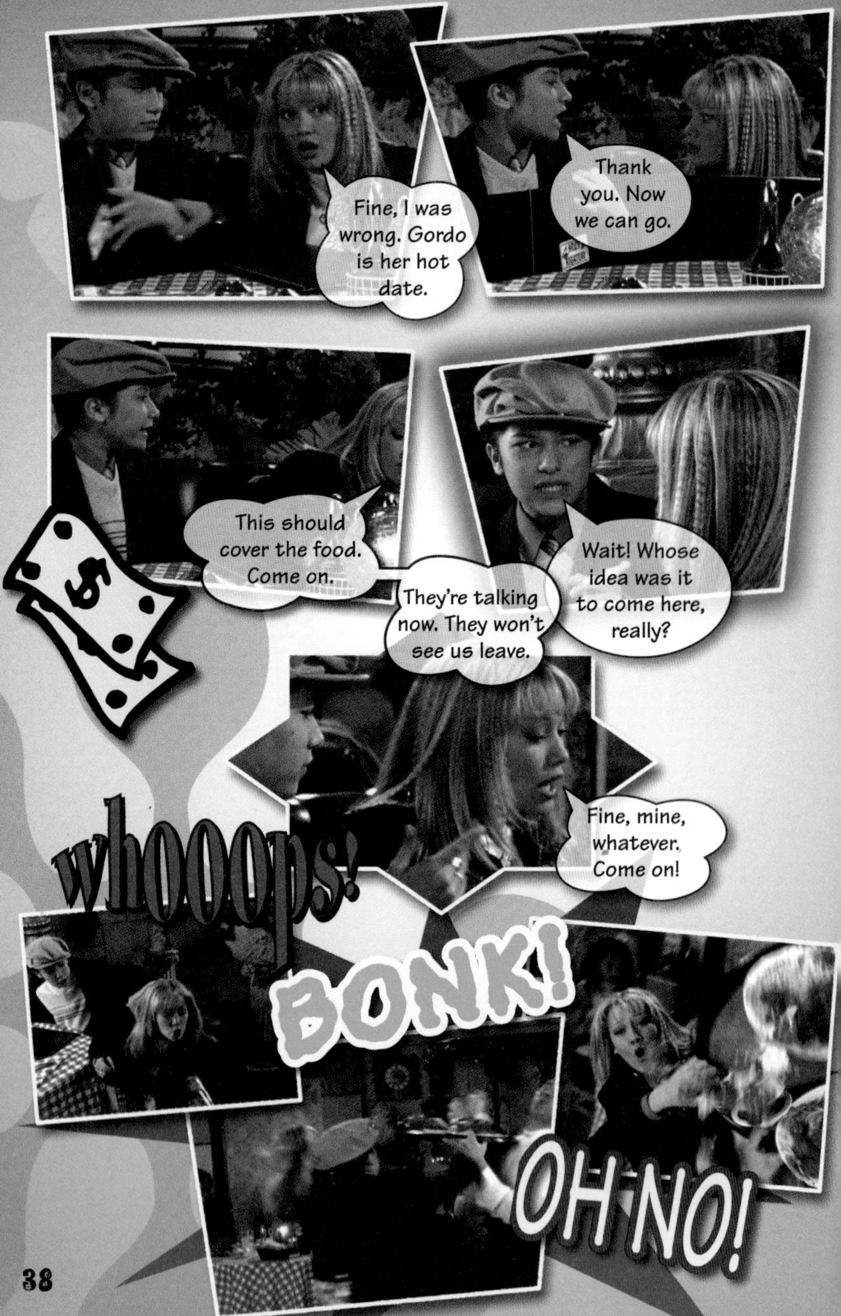
Fine, I was wrong. Gordo is her hot date.
Thank you. Now we can go.
This should cover the food. Come on.
$5
They're talking now. They won't see us leave.
Wait! Whose idea was it to come here, really?
Fine, mine, whatever. Come on!
whOOOps!
BONK!
OH NO!

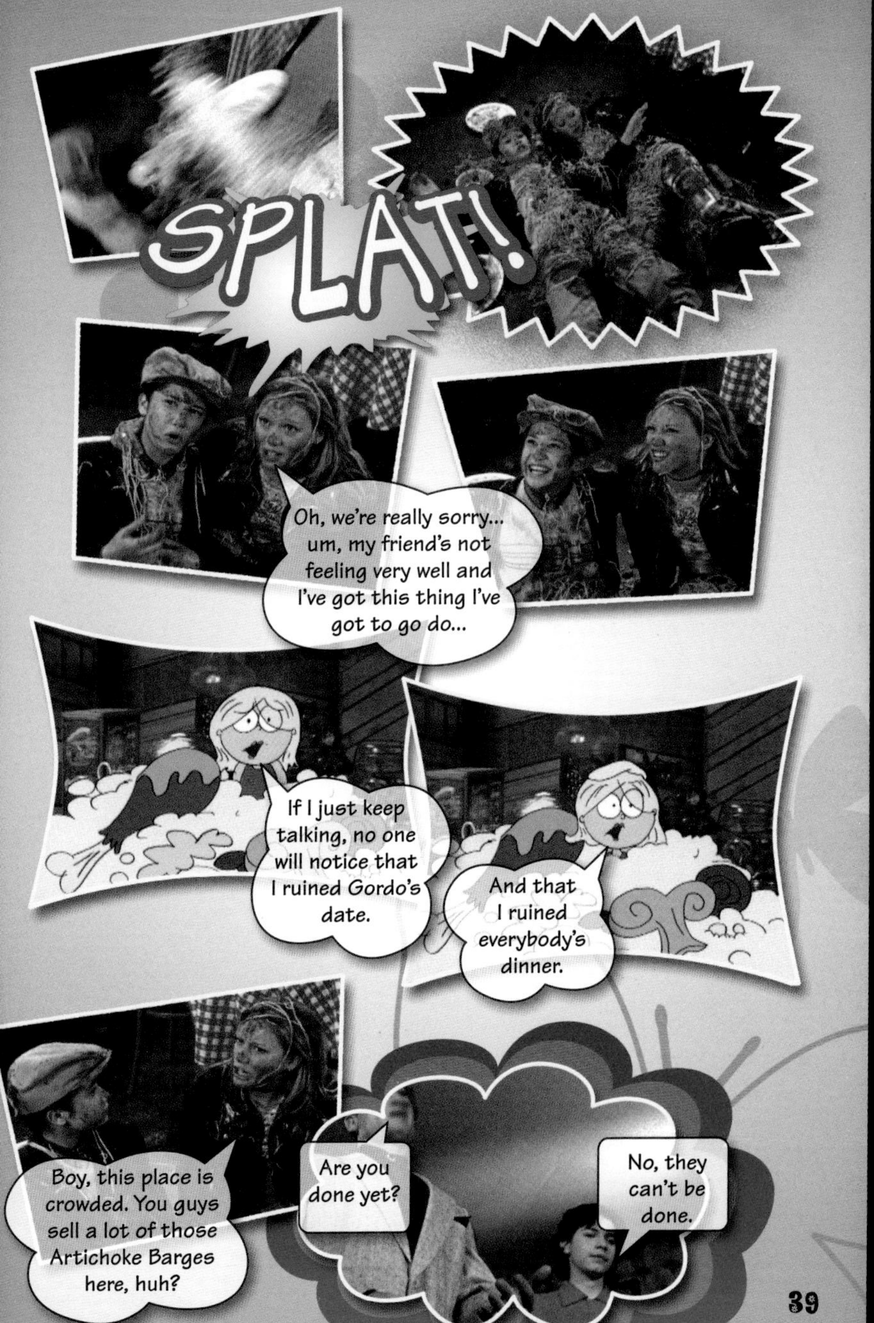
SPLAT!
Oh, we're really sorry... um, my friend's not feeling very well and I've got this thing I've got to go do...
If I just keep talking, no one will notice that I ruined Gordo's date.
And that I ruined everybody's dinner.
Boy, this place is crowded. You guys sell a lot of those Artichoke Barges here, huh?
Are you done yet?
No, they can't be done.

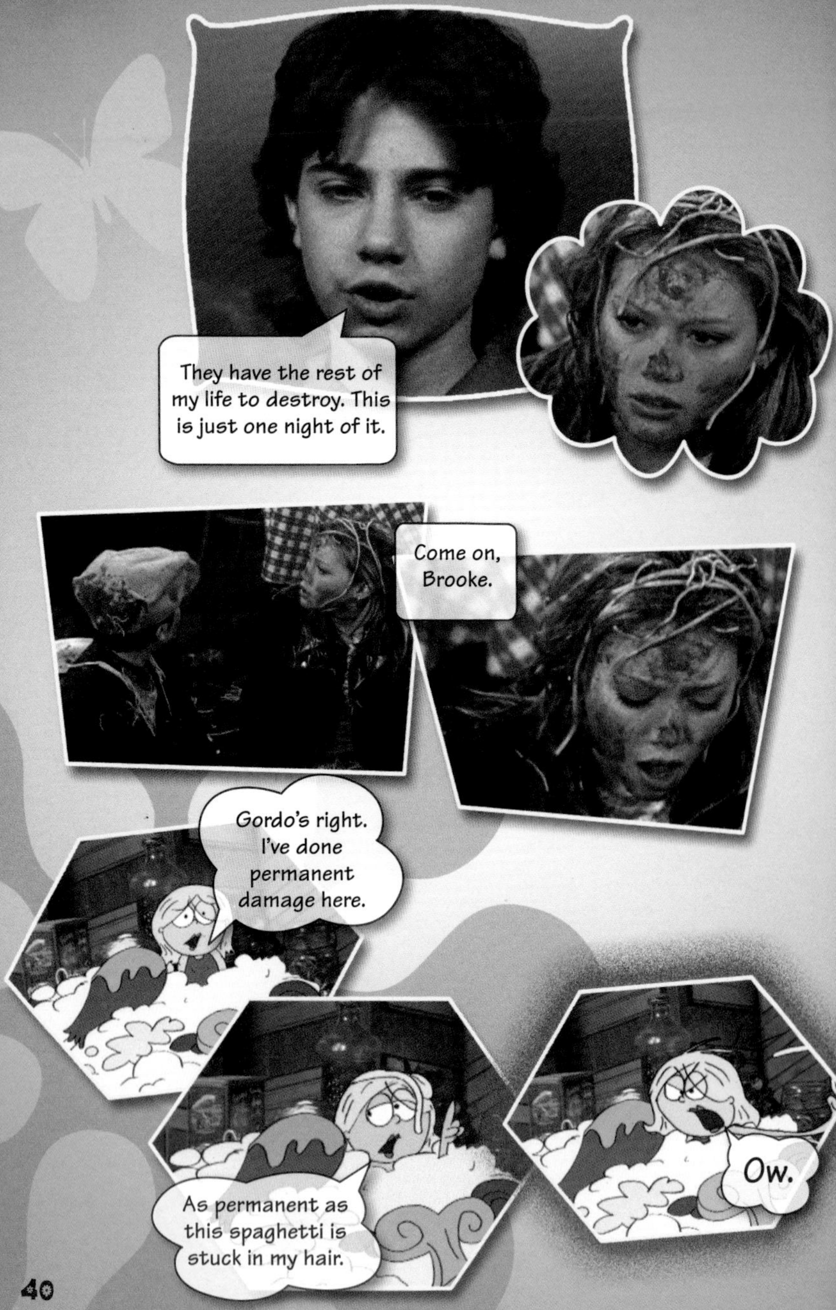
They have the rest of my life to destroy. This is just one night of it.
Come on, Brooke.
Gordo's right. I've done permanent damage here.
As permanent as this spaghetti is stuck in my hair.
Ow.

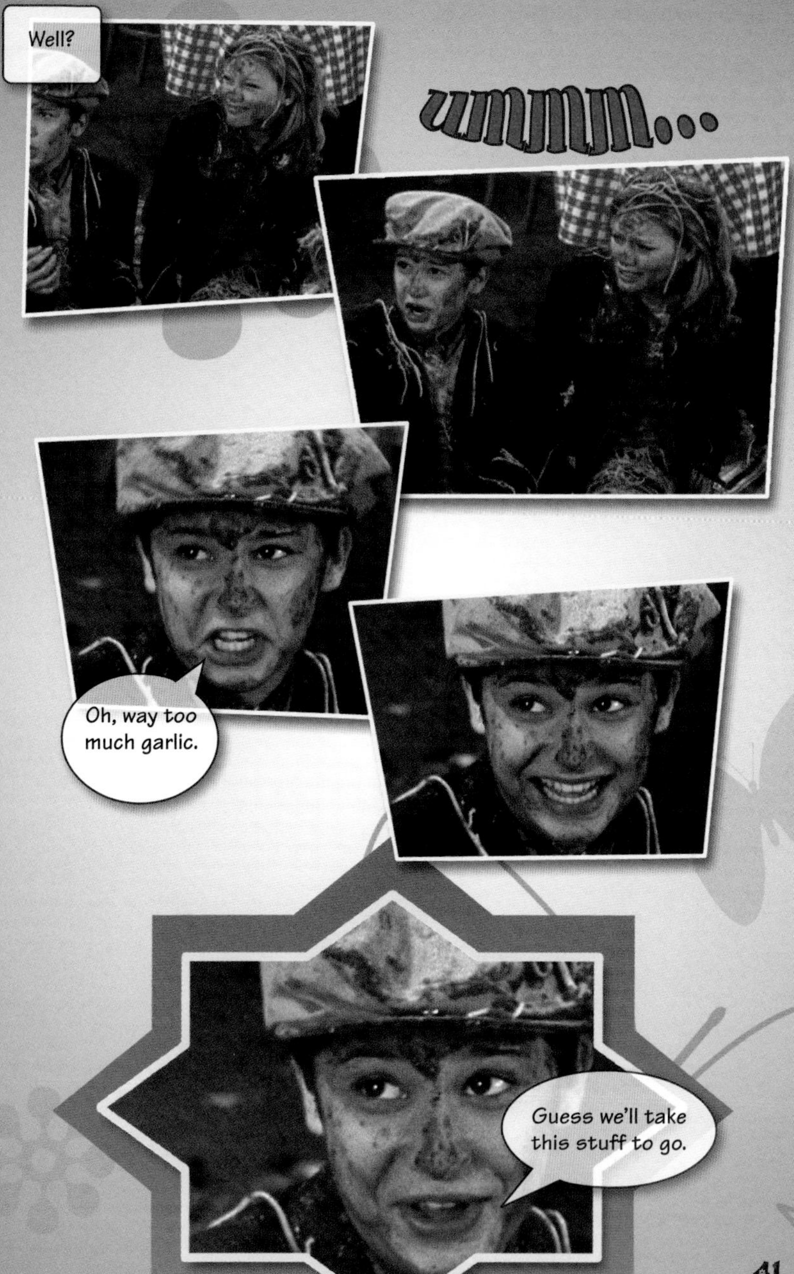
Well?
Ummmm...
Oh, way too much garlic.
Guess we'll take this stuff to go.

The next day...
If I never see another meatball again, I'll be happy.
Do you know how long it took me to wash the smell of garlic out of my hair?
I guess it's just the two of us now. No more Gordo.
No more Gordo.
No more long lectures about how we care too much about what other people think about us.
No more useless information about stuff we never even cared about in the first place.
No more packs of cupcakes to share.
No more cupcakes.
Wait, why not?

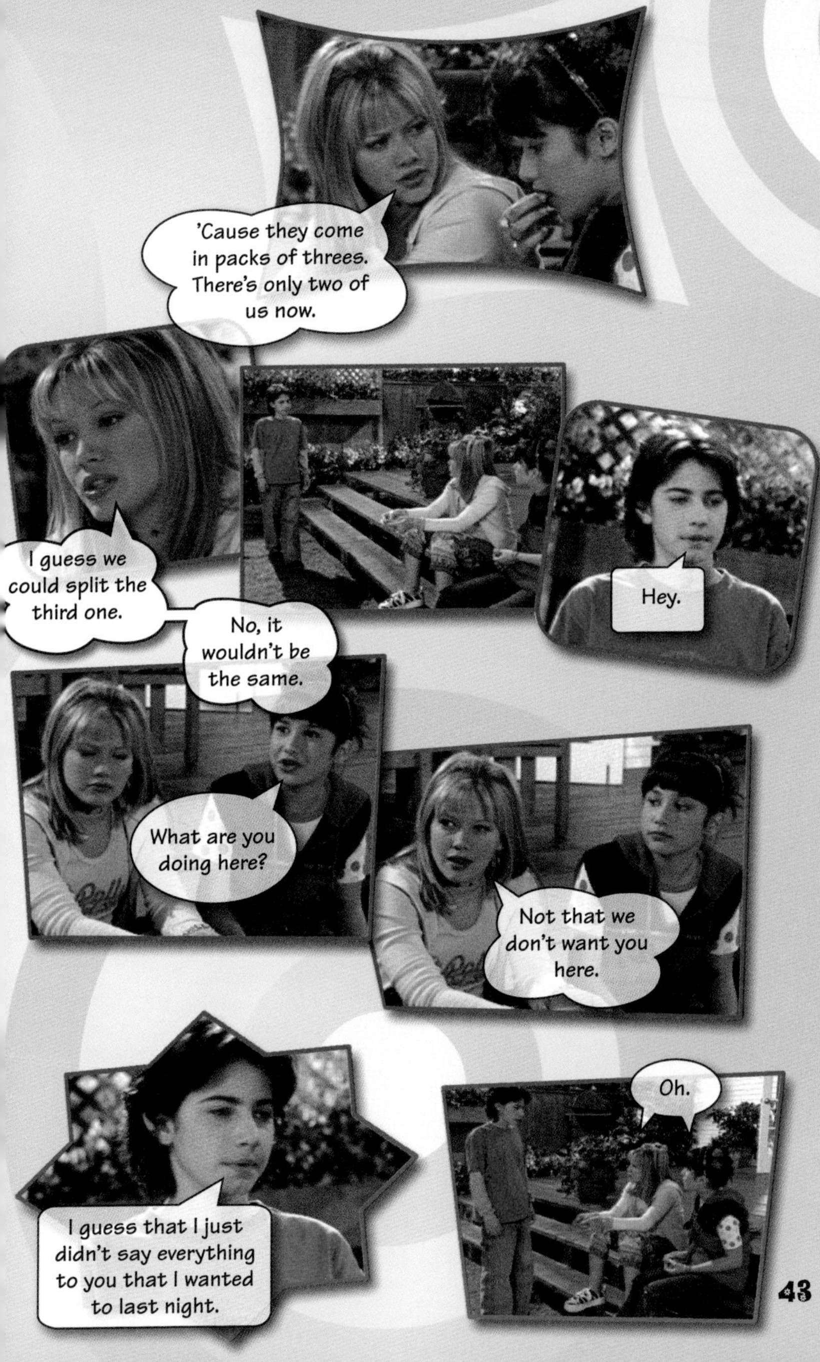
'Cause they come in packs of threes. There's only two of us now.
I guess we could split the third one.
No, it wouldn't be the same.
Hey.
What are you doing here?
Not that we don't want you here.
I guess that I just didn't say everything to you that I wanted to last night.
Oh.

Honestly? I can't believe you guys would go so far as to spy on me and Brooke. That's just really, really low. Especially for you.
It was Miranda's idea.
Lizzie!
And I also can't believe that you guys spied on me.
You just said that, Gordo.
On the one hand, I'm really insulted. But on the other hand, I realize that you guys did it because you care a lot about me.
Yeah, that's the one.

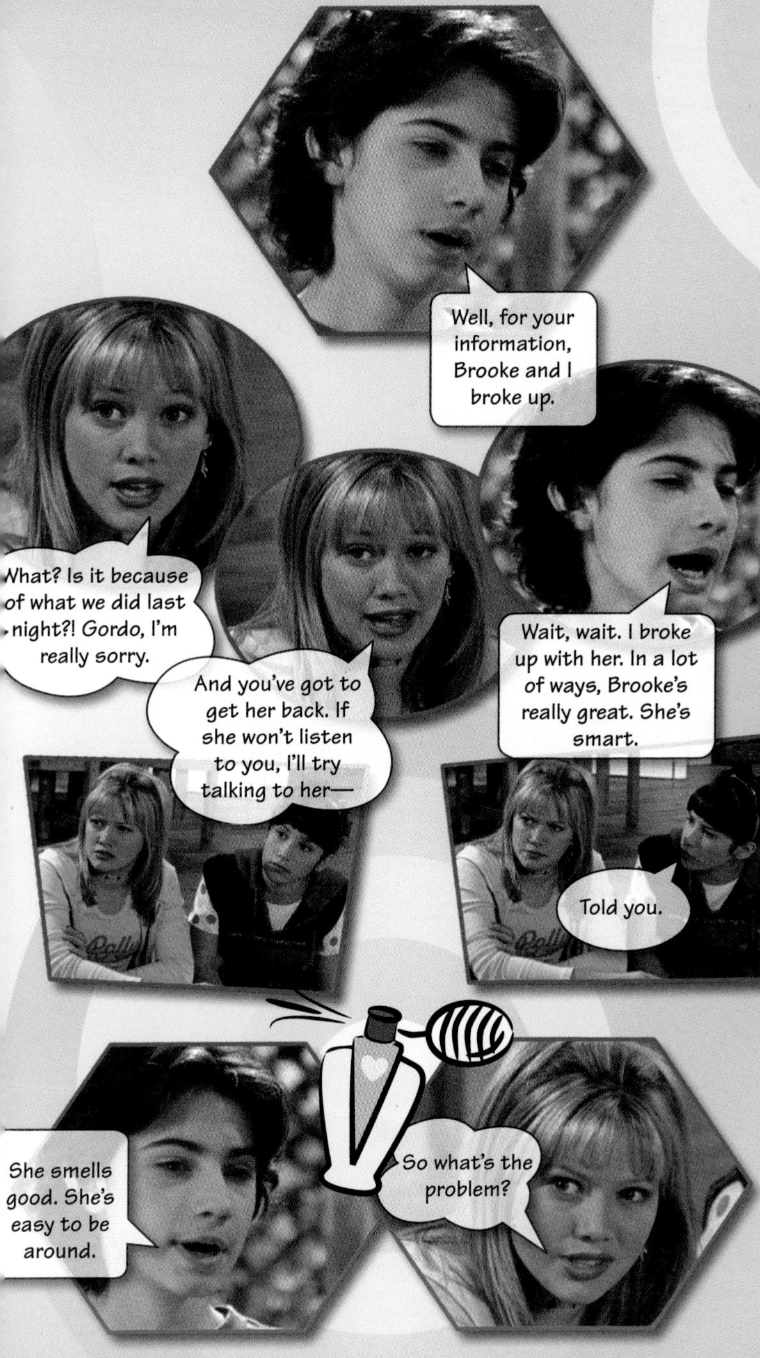
Well, for your information, Brooke and I broke up.
What? Is it because of what we did last night?! Gordo, I'm really sorry.
And you've got to get her back. If she won't listen to you, I'll try talking to her—
Wait, wait. I broke up with her. In a lot of ways, Brooke's really great. She's smart.
Told you.
She smells good. She's easy to be around.
So what's the problem?

It's kind of conceptual, but I guess I just like the idea of having a girlfriend a lot better than actually having one.
Yup. He's back.
Look, the kissing was cool, and getting notes was kind of fun. I'm just not ready for that kind of commitment.
I had to wait for her by her locker, I had to pay fo her lunches, I had no tim for myself anymore.
Bummer.
So did we.
I also had no time for you guys. I really missed that part.
I knew he'd come back. They always do.

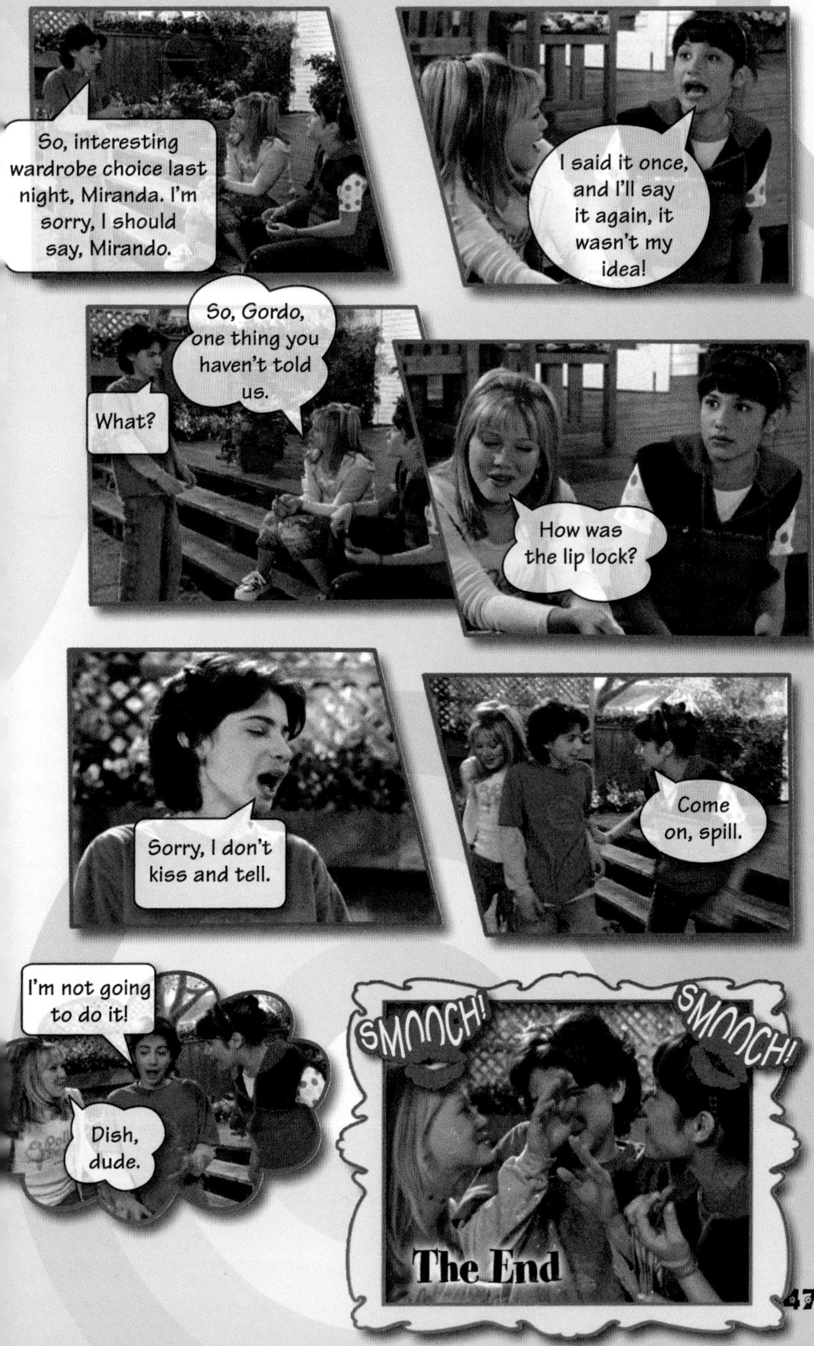
So, interesting wardrobe choice last night, Miranda. I'm sorry, I should say, Mirando.
I said it once, and I'll say it again, it wasn't my idea!
So, Gordo, one thing you haven't told us.
What?
How was the lip lock?
Sorry, I don't kiss and tell.
Come on, spill.
I'm not going to do it!
Dish, dude.
SMOOCH!
SMOOCH!
The End

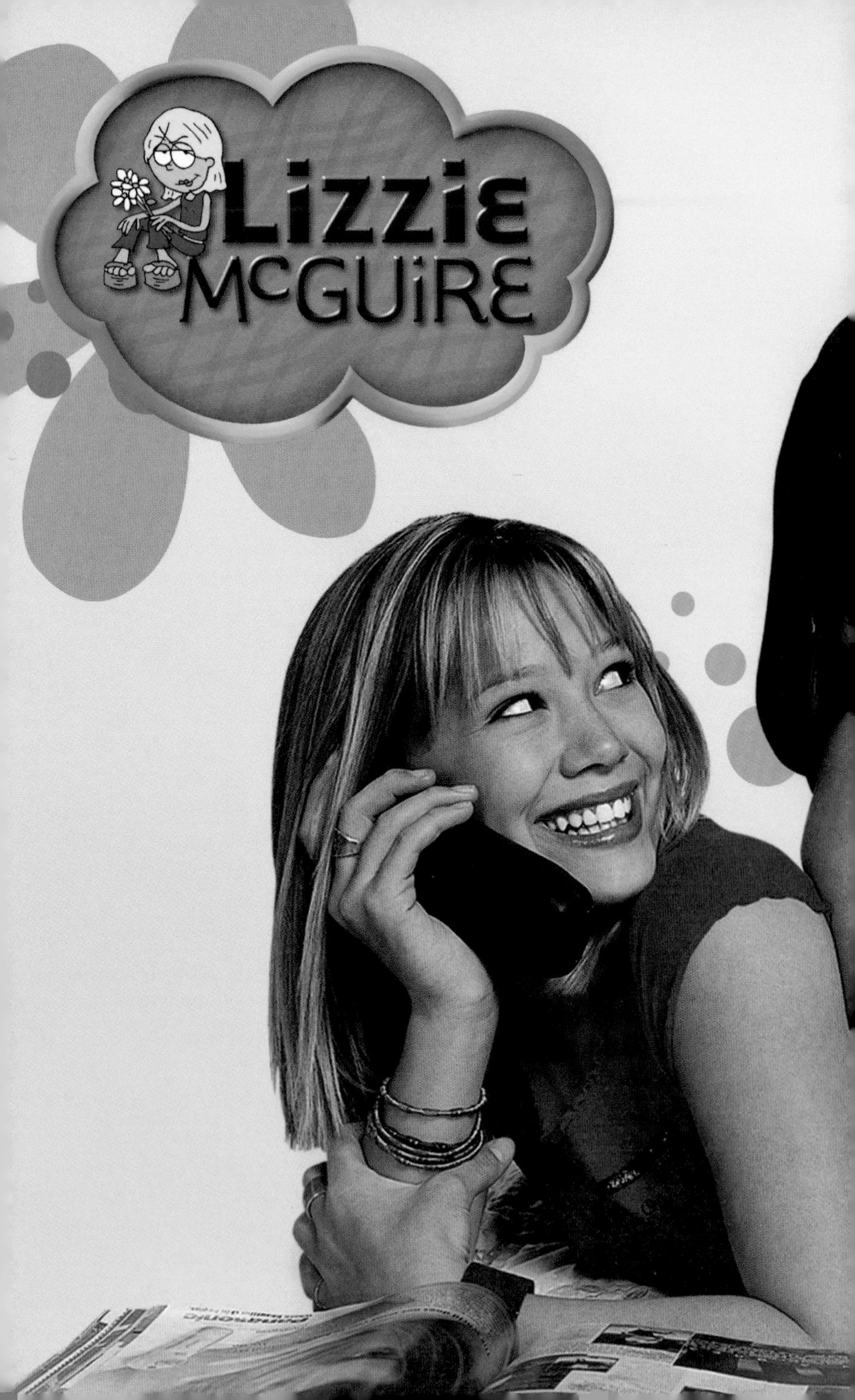
Lizzie
McGuire

You're a Good Man, Lizzie McGuire

Things get a little sticky when Lizzie and her nemesis Kate share decoration duty for the Spring Fling dance.

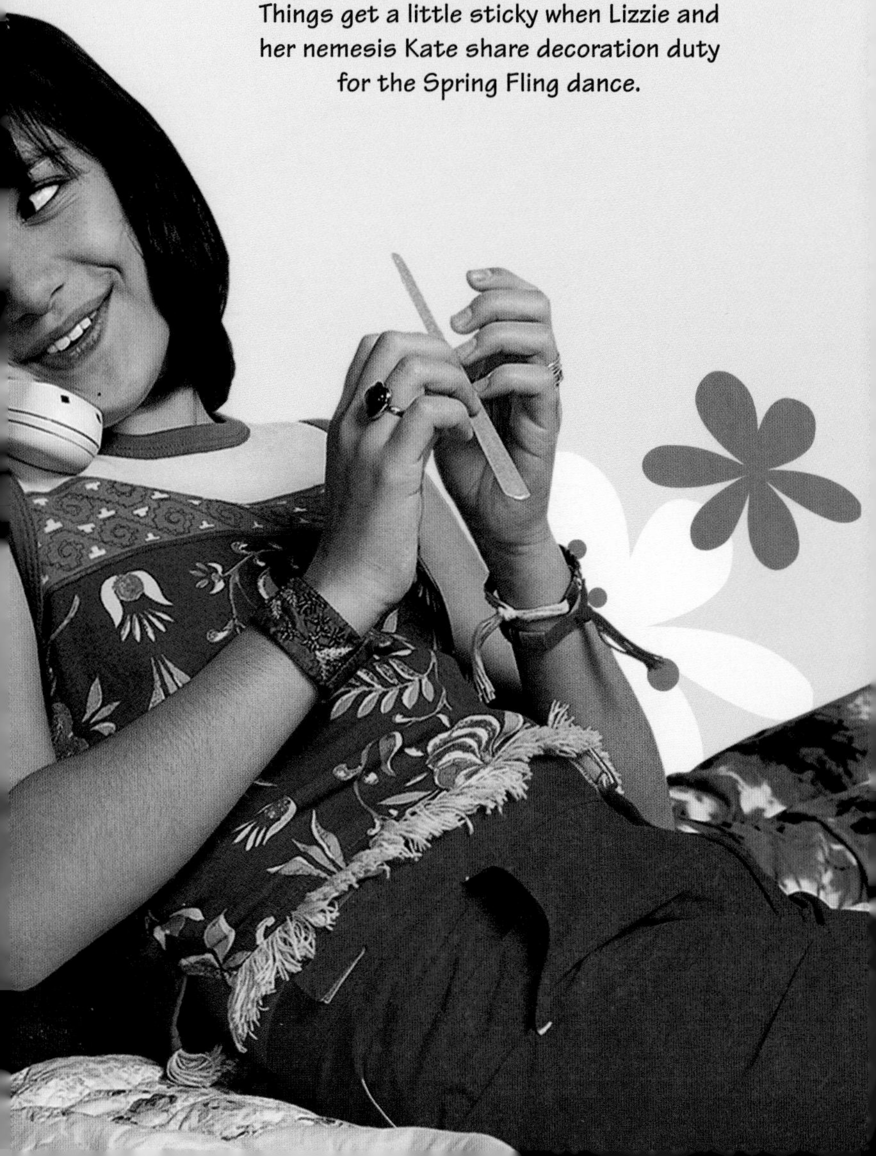

After school...

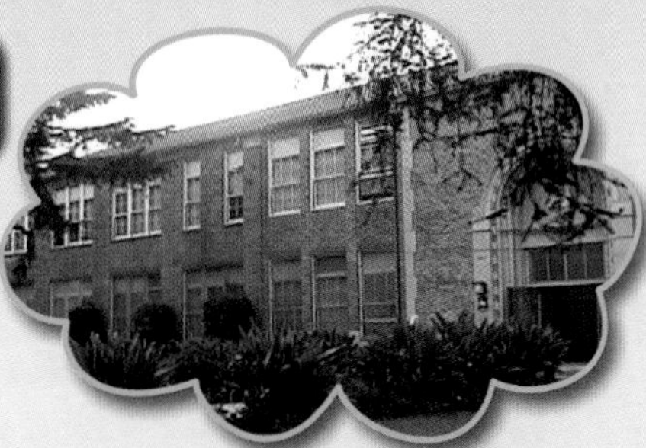

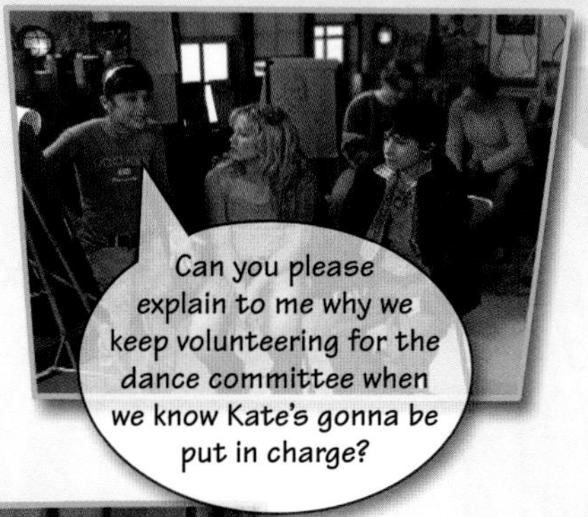
Can you please explain to me why we keep volunteering for the dance committee when we know Kate's gonna be put in charge?

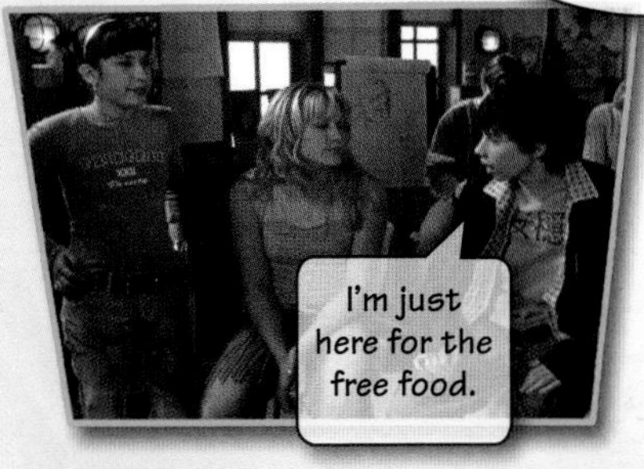
I'm just here for the free food.

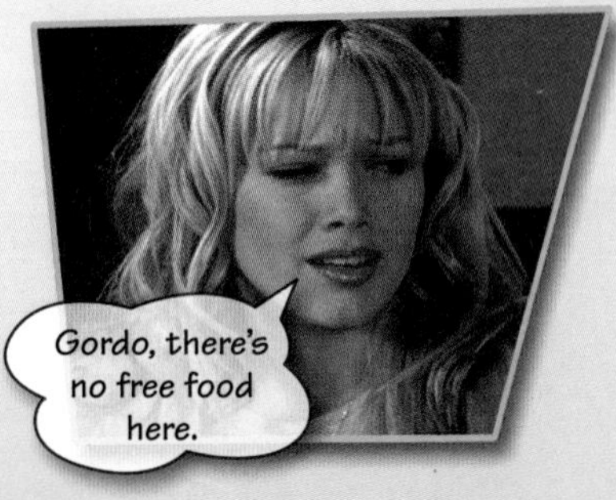
Gordo, there's no free food here.

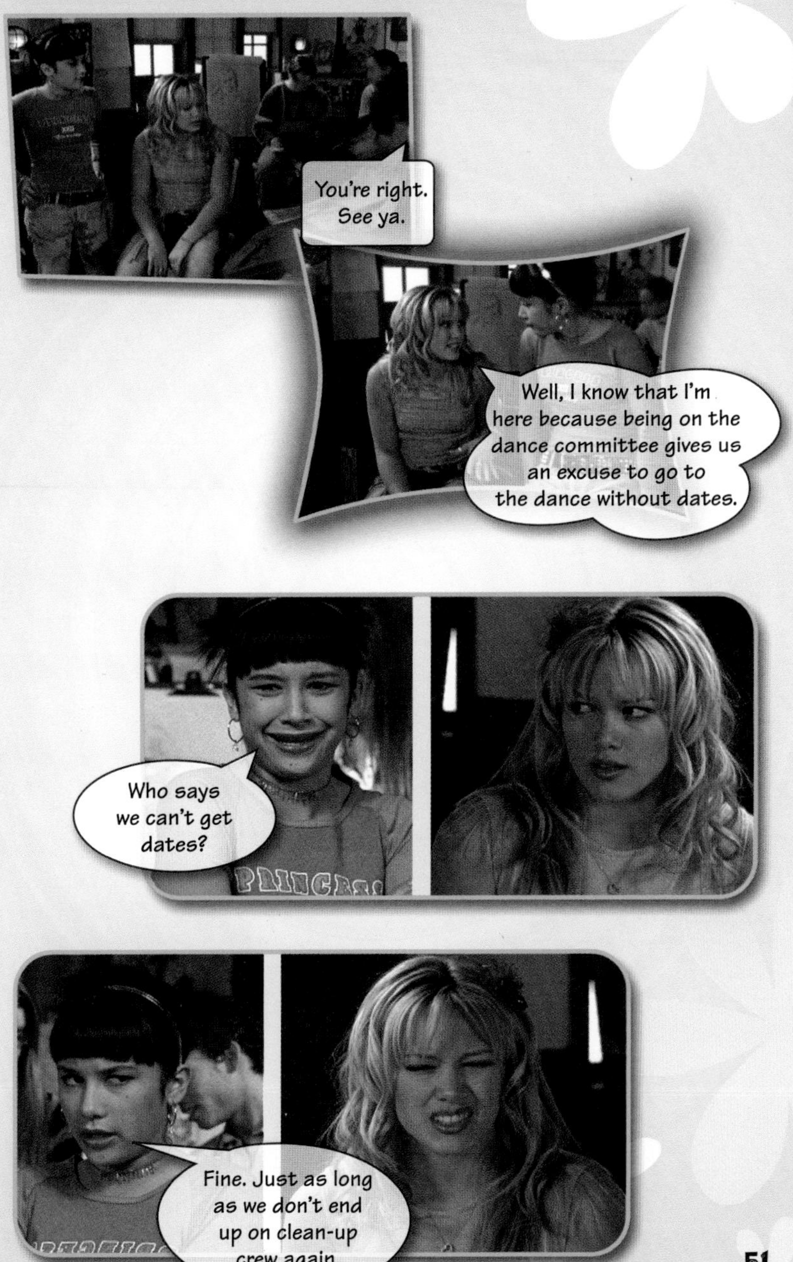
You're right. See ya.
Well, I know that I'm here because being on the dance committee gives us an excuse to go to the dance without dates.
Who says we can't get dates?
Fine. Just as long as we don't end up on clean-up crew again.

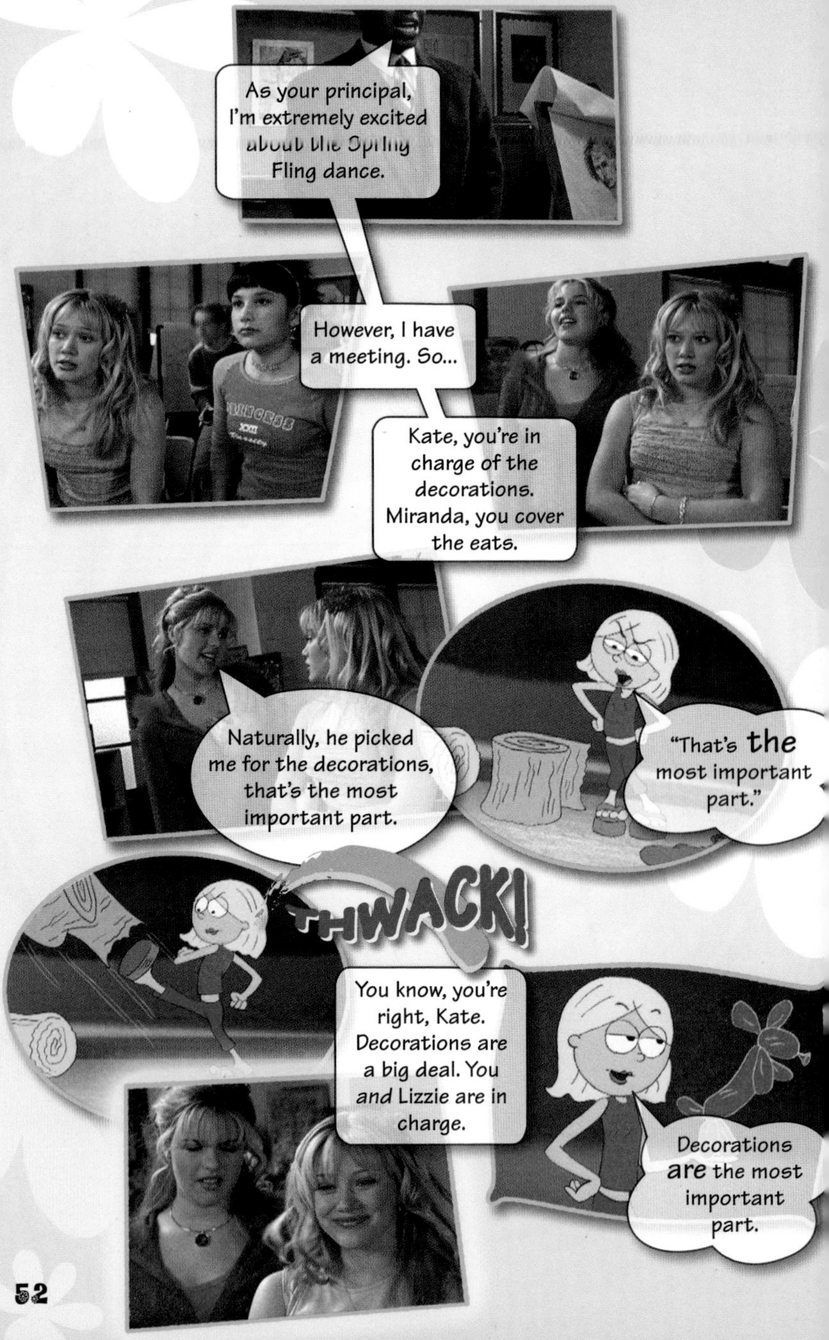
As your principal, I'm extremely excited about the Spring Fling dance.
However, I have a meeting. So...
Kate, you're in charge of the decorations. Miranda, you cover the eats.
Naturally, he picked me for the decorations, that's the most important part.
"That's the most important part."
THWACK!
You know, you're right, Kate. Decorations are a big deal. You and Lizzie are in charge.
Decorations are the most important part.

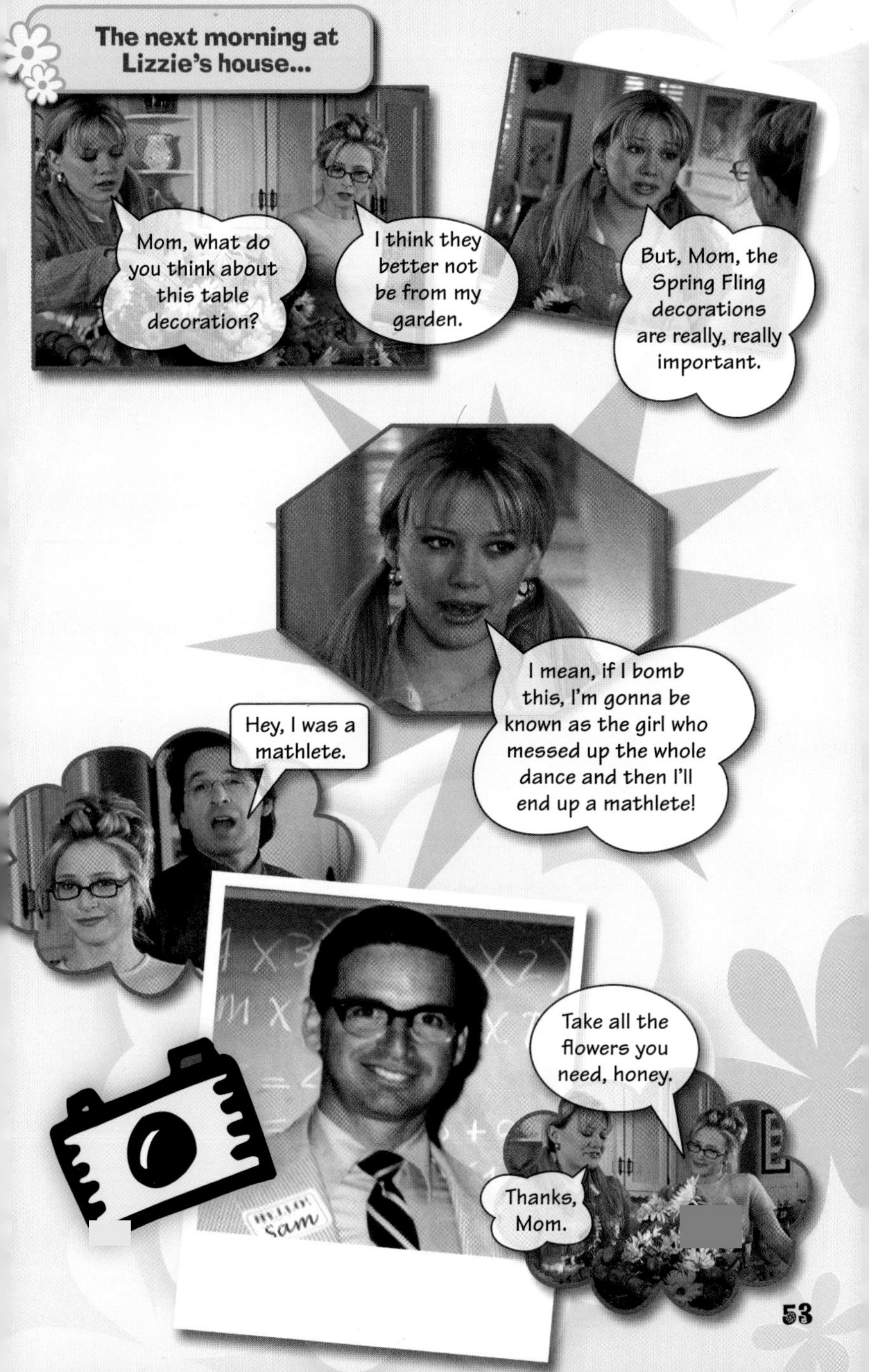
The next morning at Lizzie's house...
Mom, what do you think about this table decoration?
I think they better not be from my garden.
But, Mom, the Spring Fling decorations are really, really important.
I mean, if I bomb this, I'm gonna be known as the girl who messed up the whole dance and then I'll end up a mathlete!
Hey, I was a mathlete.
Take all the flowers you need, honey.
Thanks, Mom.

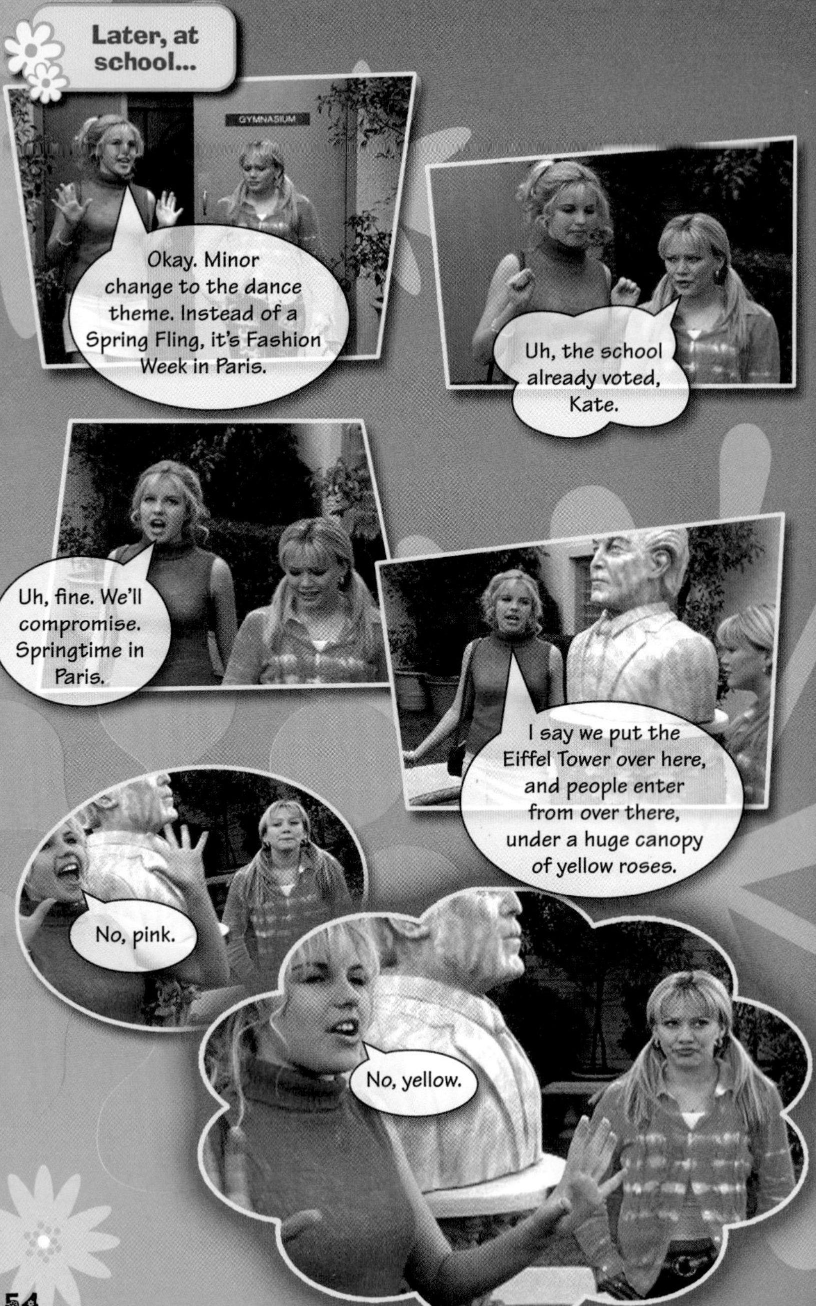
Later, at school...
GYMNASIUM
Okay. Minor change to the dance theme. Instead of a Spring Fling, it's Fashion Week in Paris.
Uh, the school already voted, Kate.
Uh, fine. We'll compromise. Springtime in Paris.
I say we put the Eiffel Tower over here, and people enter from over there, under a huge canopy of yellow roses.
No, pink.
No, yellow.

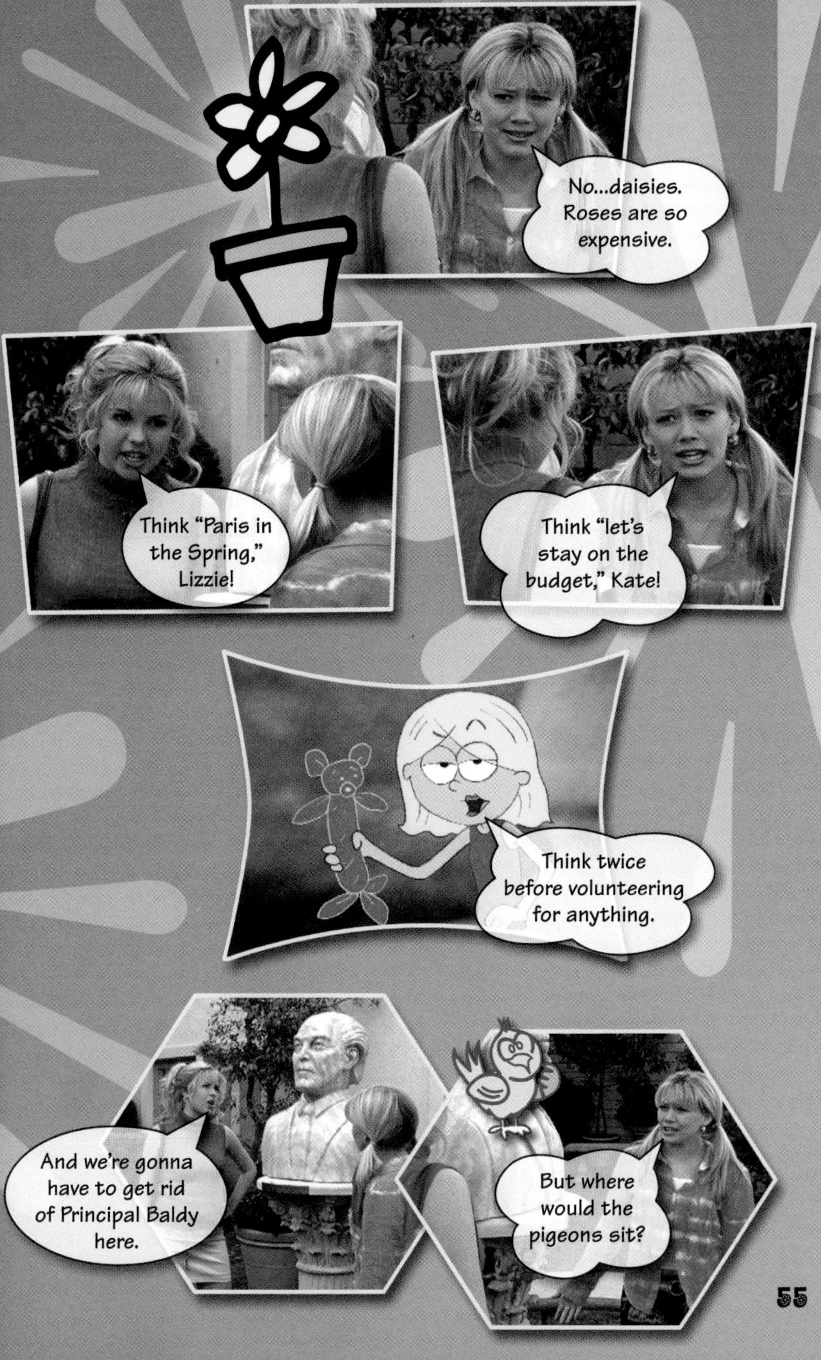
No...daisies. Roses are so expensive.
Think "Paris in the Spring," Lizzie!
Think "let's stay on the budget," Kate!
Think twice before volunteering for anything.
And we're gonna have to get rid of Principal Baldy here.
But where would the pigeons sit?

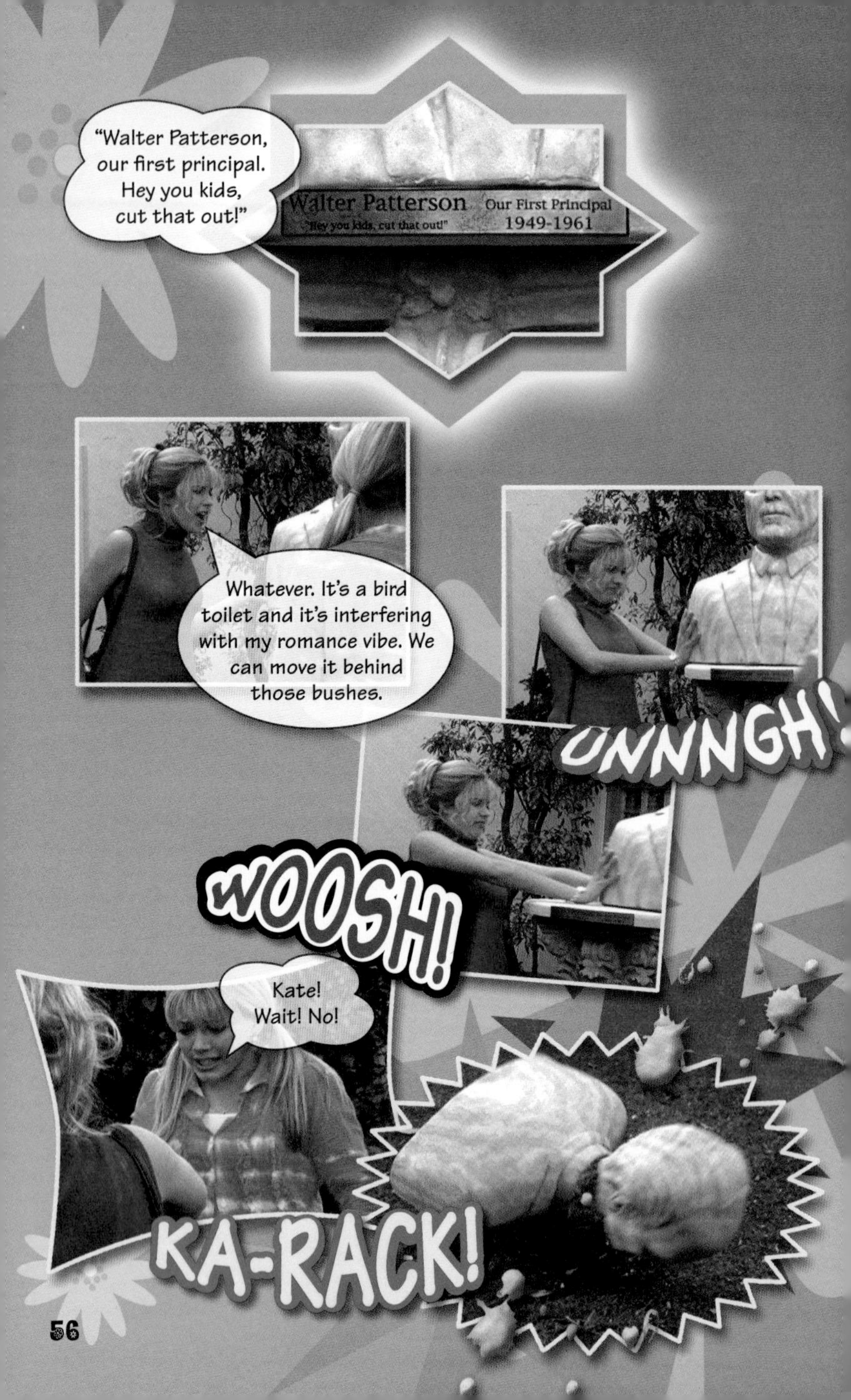
"Walter Patterson, our first principal. Hey you kids, cut that out!"
Walter Patterson
"Hey you kids, cut that out!"
Our First Principal
1949-1961
Whatever. It's a bird toilet and it's interfering with my romance vibe. We can move it behind those bushes.
UNNNGH!
WOOSH!
Kate! Wait! No!
KA-RACK!

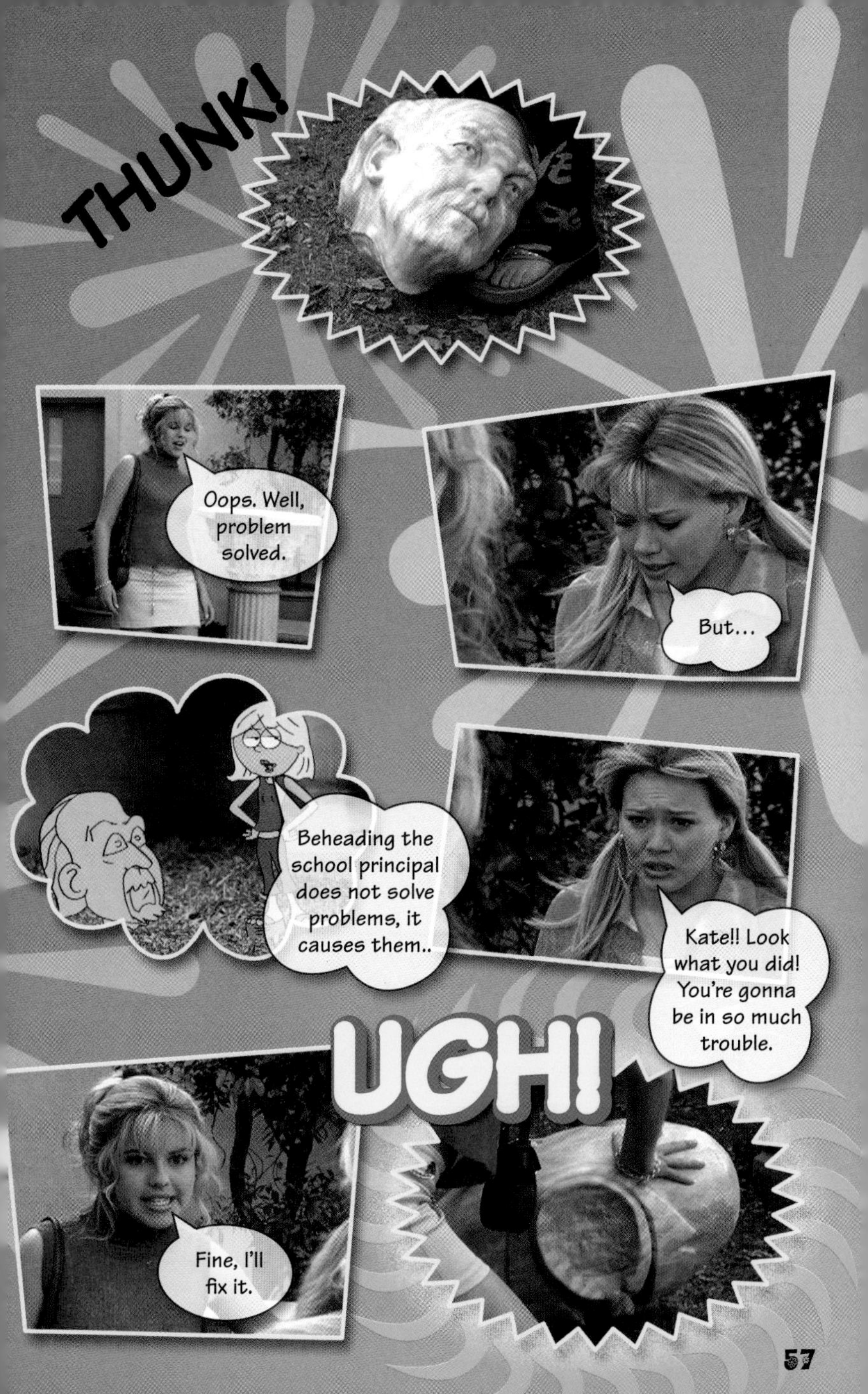

THUNK!
Oops. Well, problem solved.
But...
Beheading the school principal does not solve problems, it causes them..
Kate!! Look what you did! You're gonna be in so much trouble.
UGH!
Fine, I'll fix it.

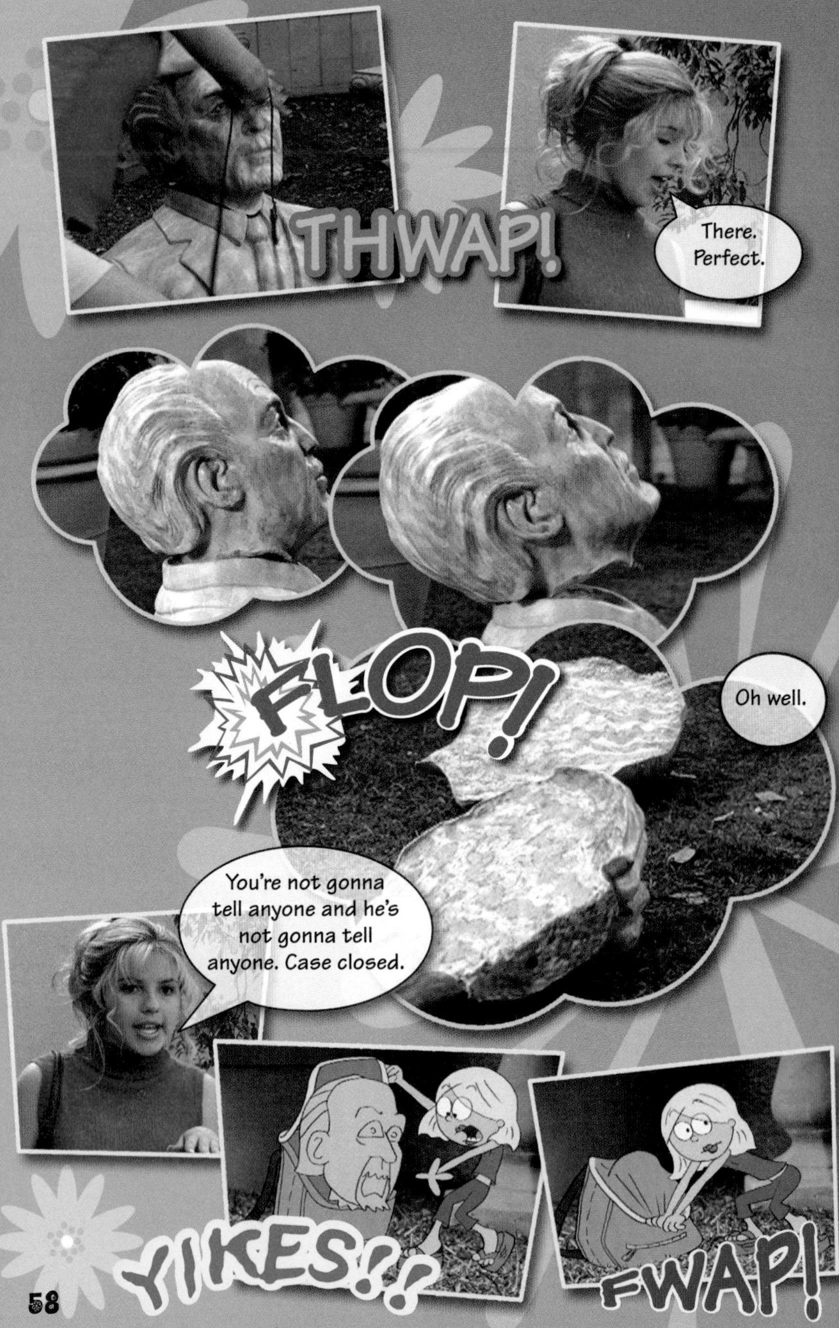
THWAP!
There. Perfect.
FLOP!
Oh well.
You're not gonna tell anyone and he's not gonna tell anyone. Case closed.
YIKES!?!
FWAP!

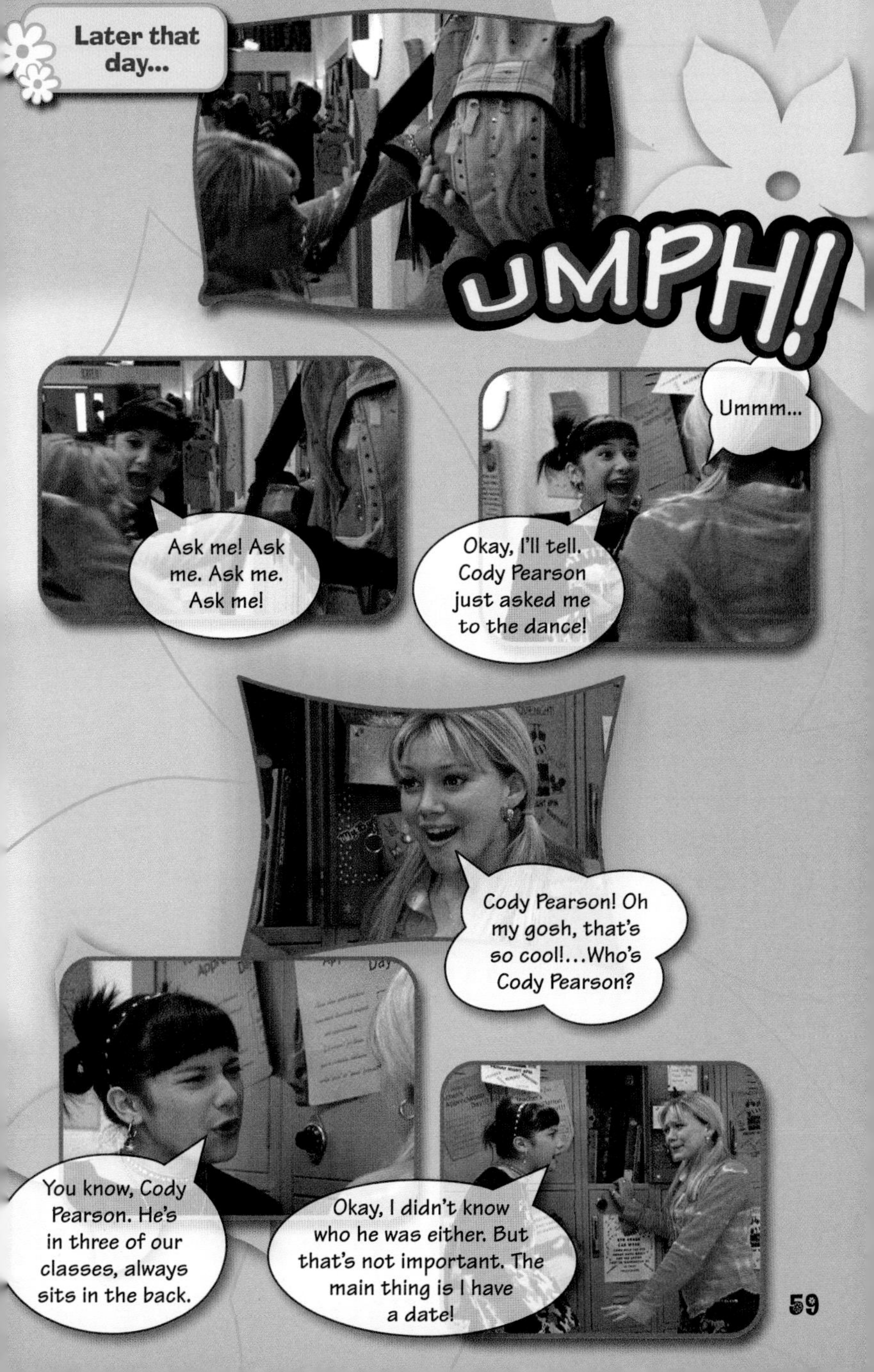
Later that day...
UMPH!
Ask me! Ask me. Ask me. Ask me!
Ummm...
Okay, I'll tell. Cody Pearson just asked me to the dance!
Cody Pearson! Oh my gosh, that's so cool!...Who's Cody Pearson?
You know, Cody Pearson. He's in three of our classes, always sits in the back.
Okay, I didn't know who he was either. But that's not important. The main thing is I have a date!

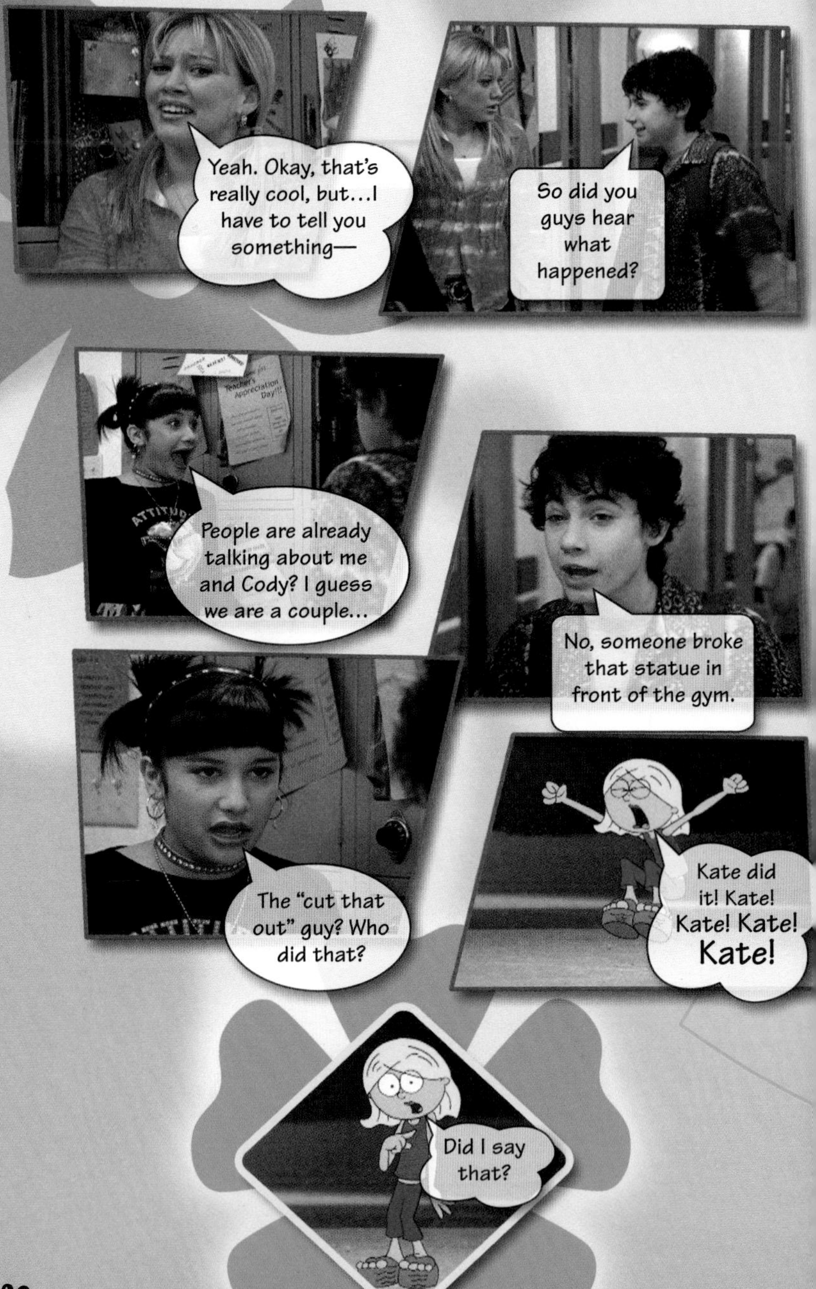
Yeah. Okay, that's really cool, but…I have to tell you something—
So did you guys hear what happened?
People are already talking about me and Cody? I guess we are a couple…
No, someone broke that statue in front of the gym.
The "cut that out" guy? Who did that?
Kate did it! Kate! Kate! Kate! Kate!
Did I say that?

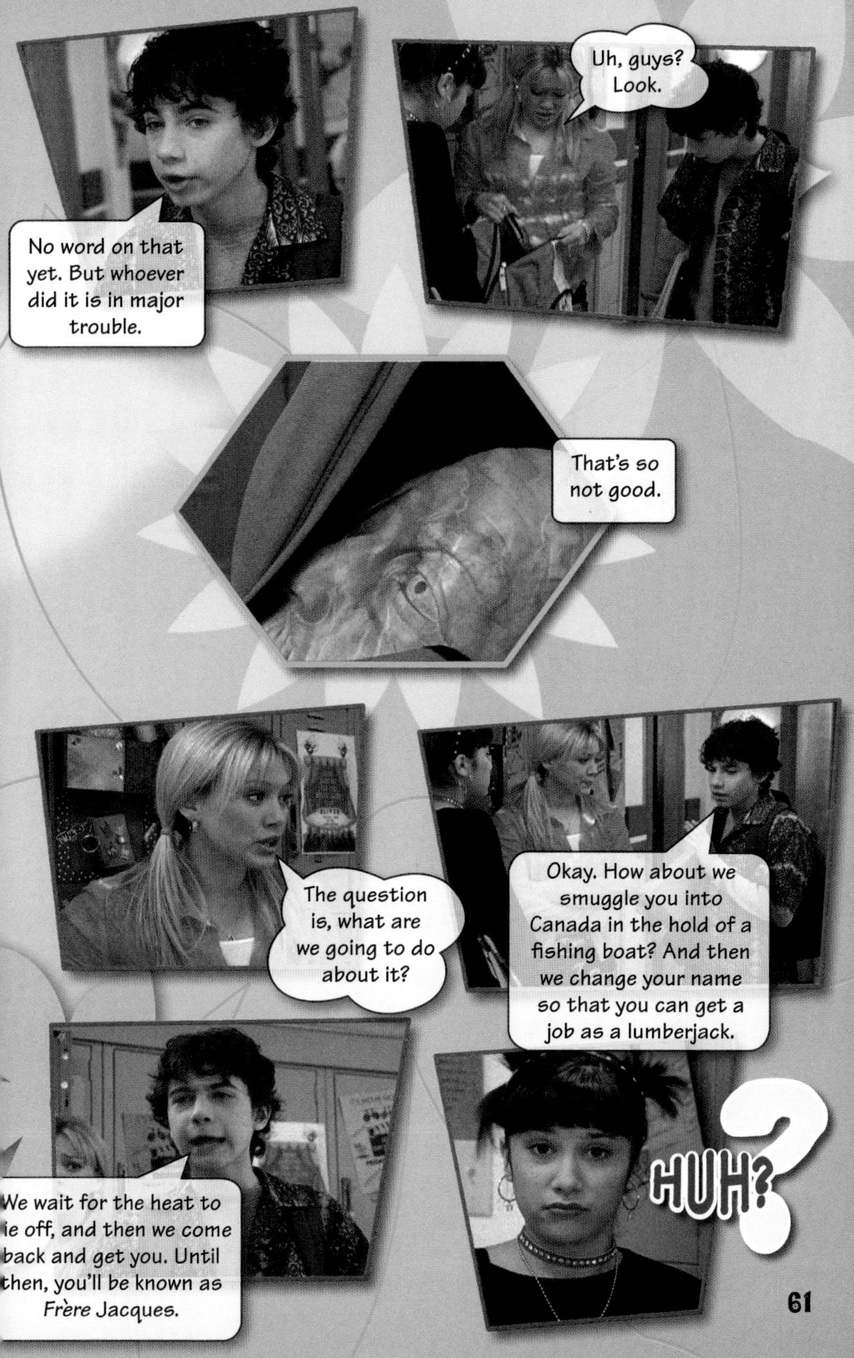

No word on that yet. But whoever did it is in major trouble.
Uh, guys? Look.
That's so not good.
The question is, what are we going to do about it?
Okay. How about we smuggle you into Canada in the hold of a fishing boat? And then we change your name so that you can get a job as a lumberjack.
We wait for the heat to ie off, and then we come back and get you. Until then, you'll be known as Frère Jacques.
HUH?

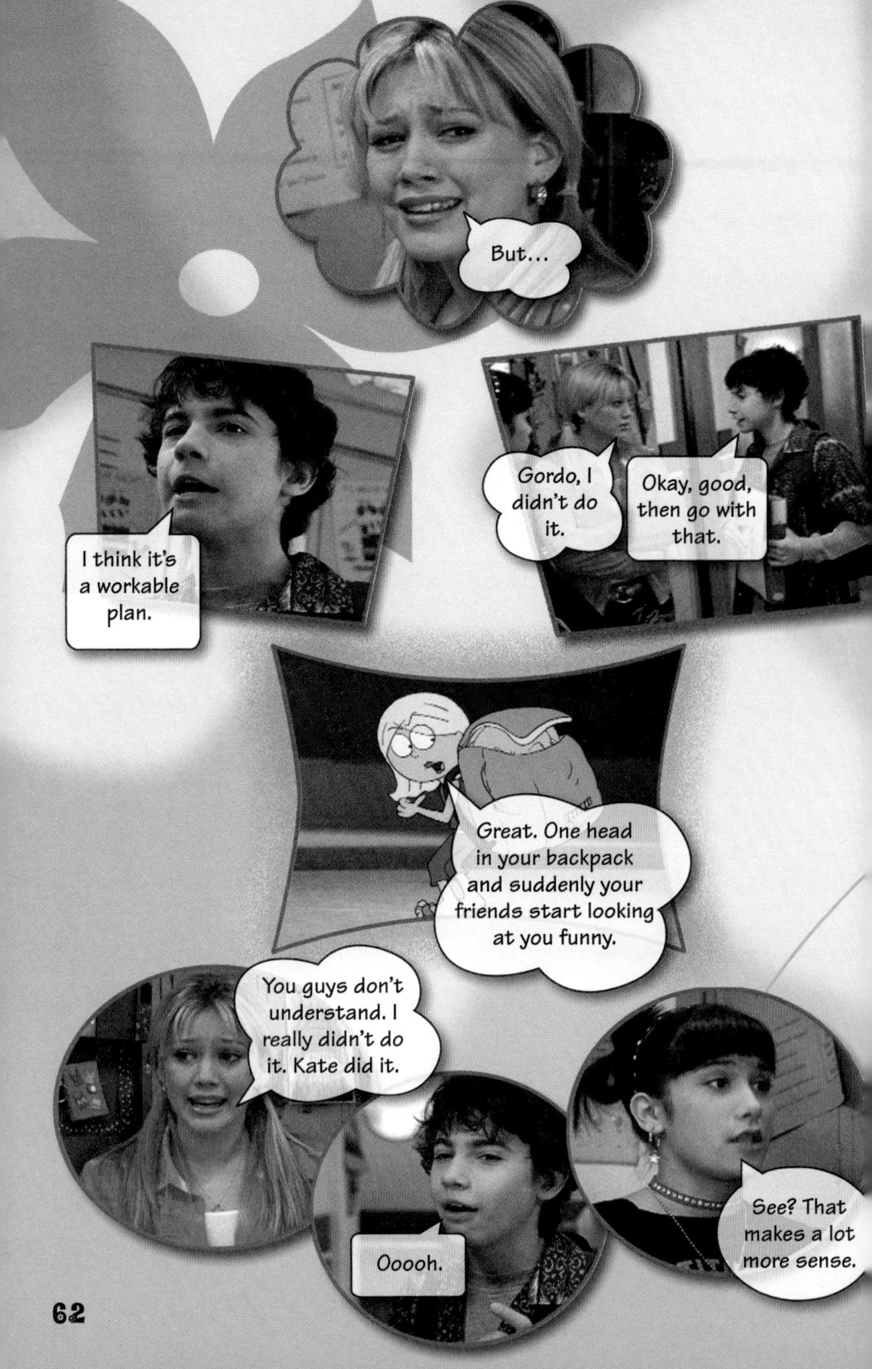

But...
I think it's a workable plan.
Gordo, I didn't do it.
Okay, good, then go with that.
Great. One head in your backpack and suddenly your friends start looking at you funny.
You guys don't understand. I really didn't do it. Kate did it.
Ooooh.
See? That makes a lot more sense.

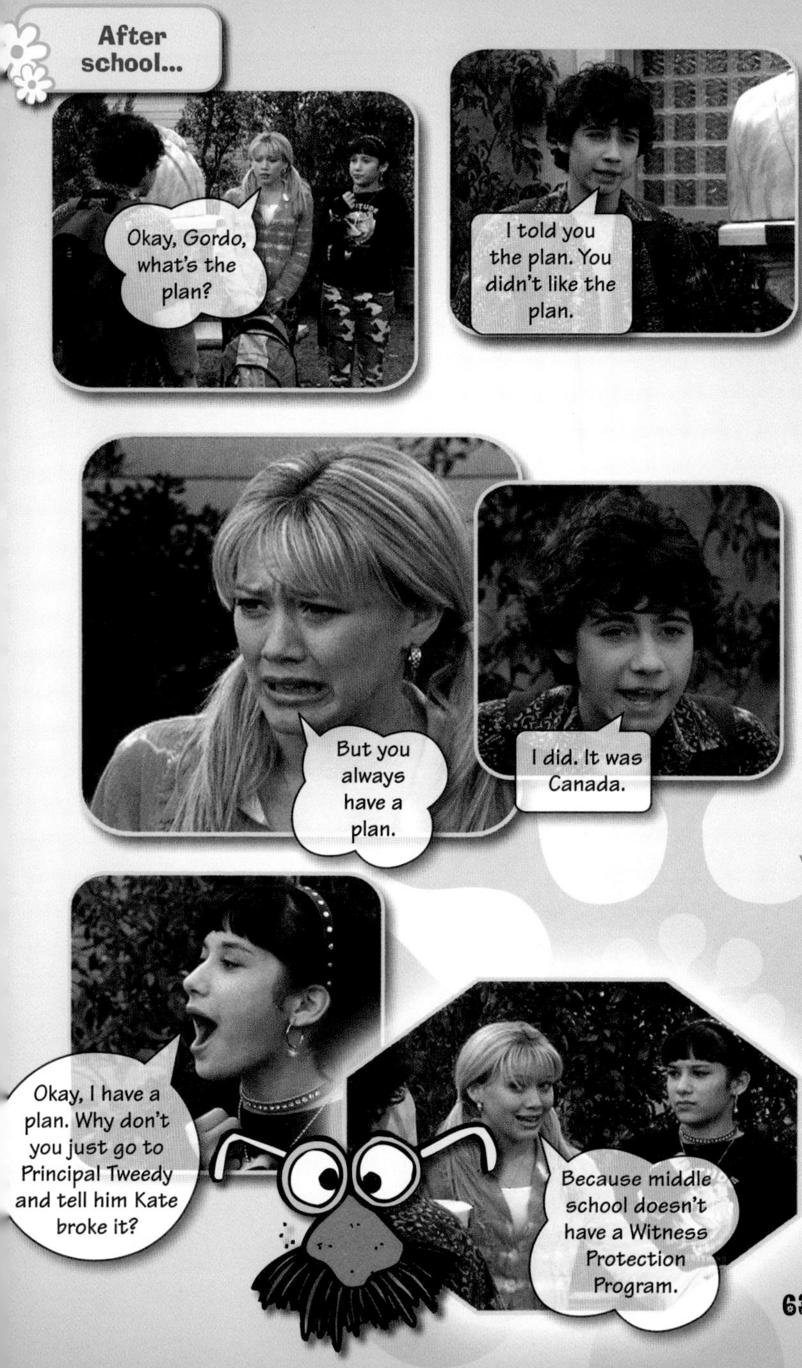
After school...
Okay, Gordo, what's the plan?
I told you the plan. You didn't like the plan.
But you always have a plan.
I did. It was Canada.
Okay, I have a plan. Why don't you just go to Principal Tweedy and tell him Kate broke it?
Because middle school doesn't have a Witness Protection Program.

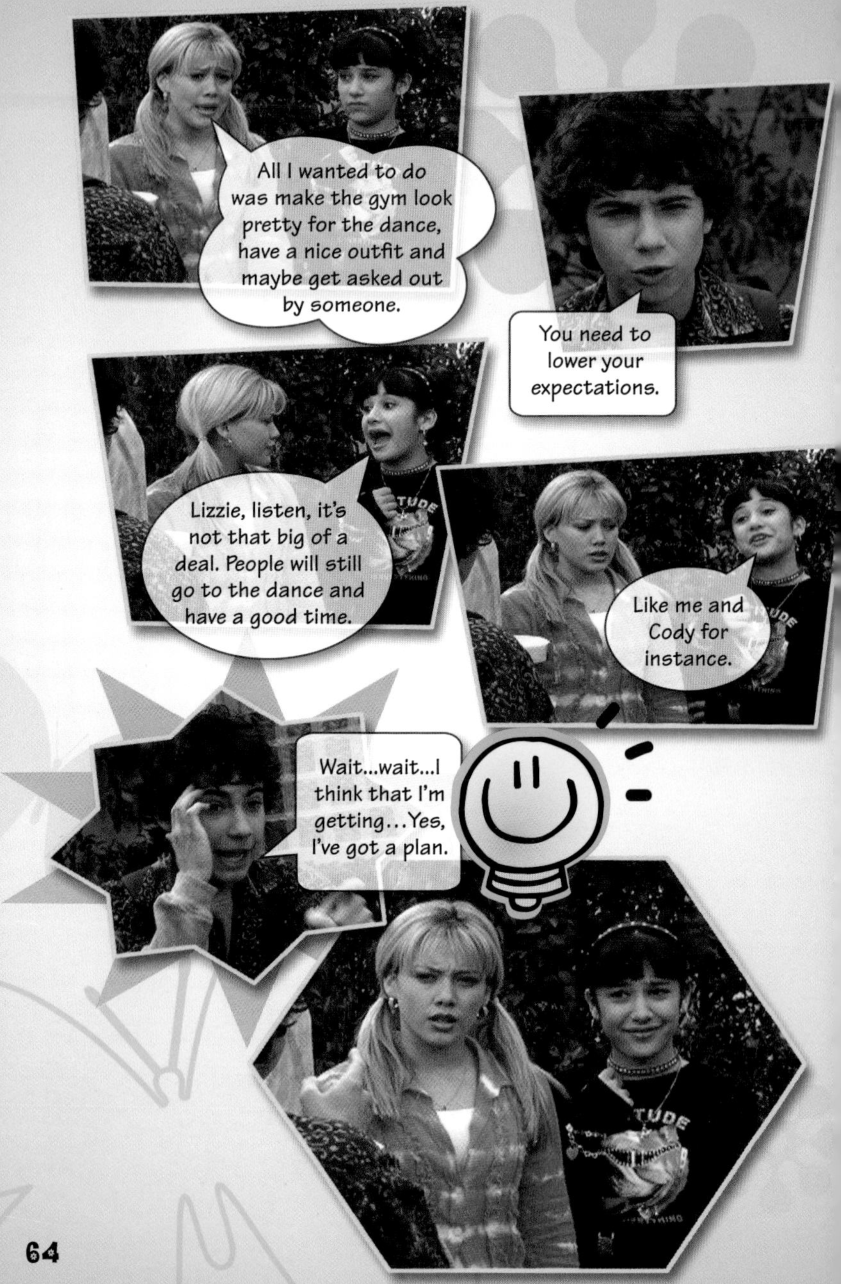
All I wanted to do was make the gym look pretty for the dance, have a nice outfit and maybe get asked out by someone.
You need to lower your expectations.
Lizzie, listen, it's not that big of a deal. People will still go to the dance and have a good time.
Like me and Cody for instance.
Wait...wait...I think that I'm getting…Yes, I've got a plan.

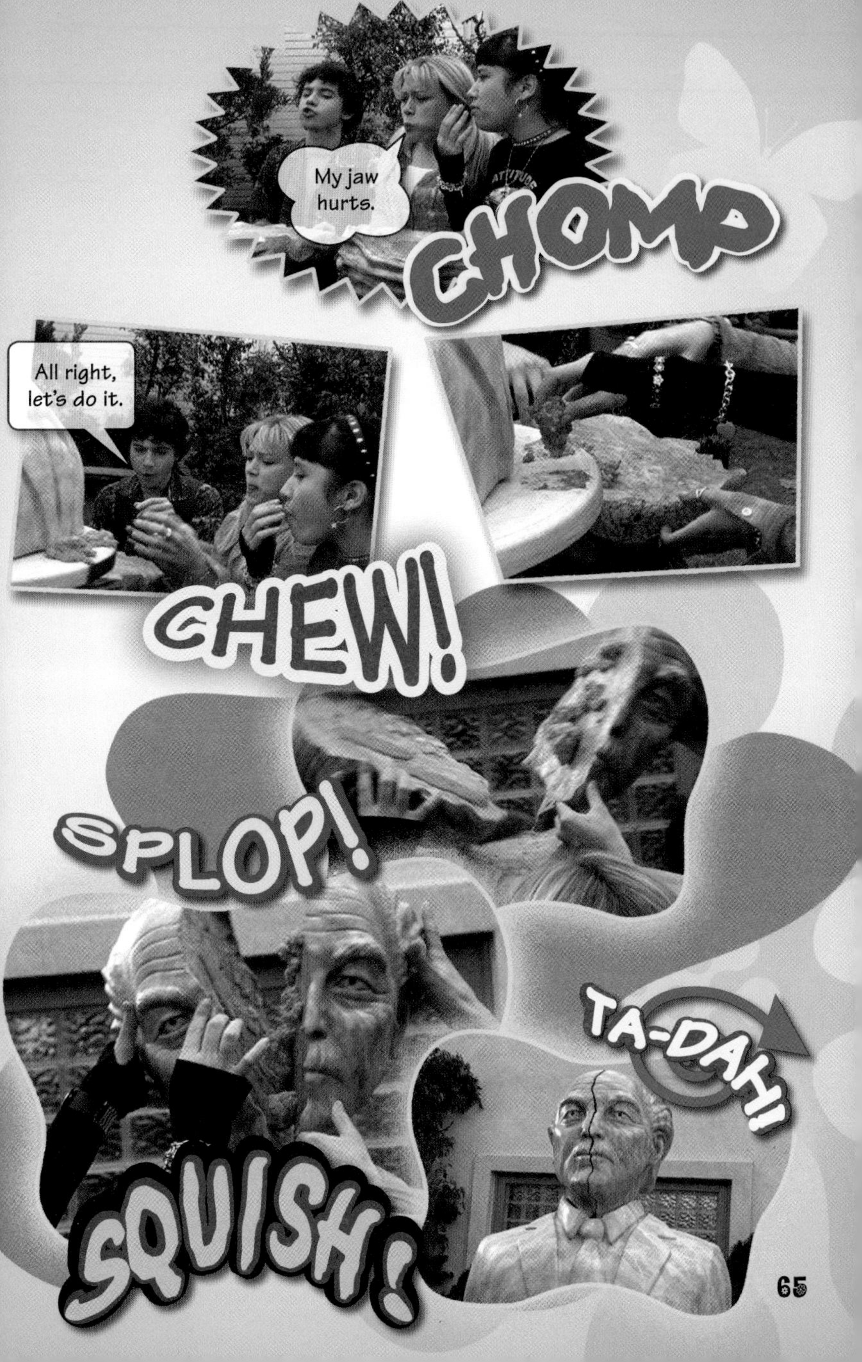
My jaw hurts.
CHOMP
All right, let's do it.
CHEW!
SPLOP!
SQUISH!
TA-DAH!

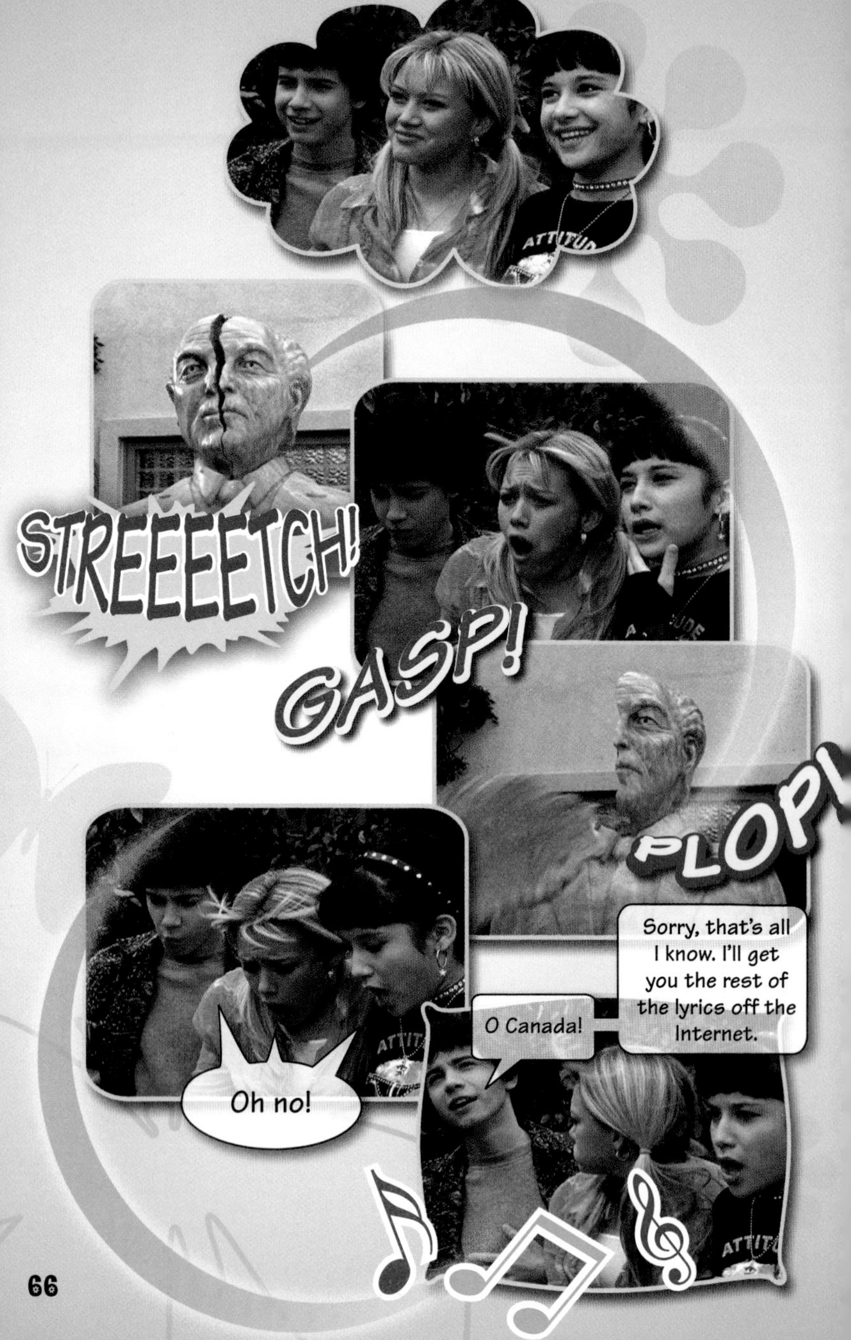
STREEEETCH!
GASP!
PLOP!
Oh no!
O Canada!
Sorry, that's all I know. I'll get you the rest of the lyrics off the Internet.

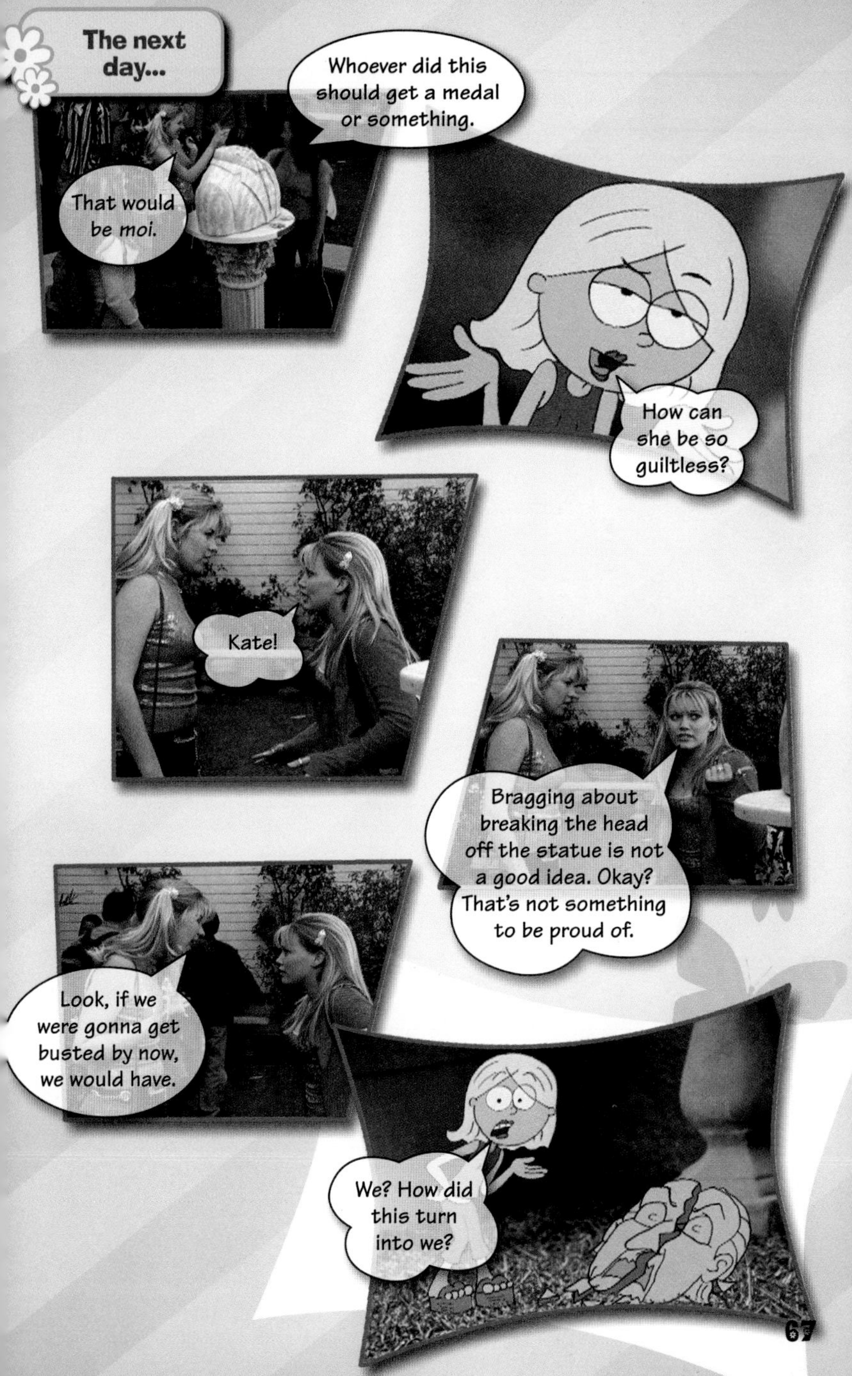
The next day...
Whoever did this should get a medal or something.
That would be moi.
How can she be so guiltless?
Kate!
Bragging about breaking the head off the statue is not a good idea. Okay? That's not something to be proud of.
Look, if we were gonna get busted by now, we would have.
We? How did this turn into we?

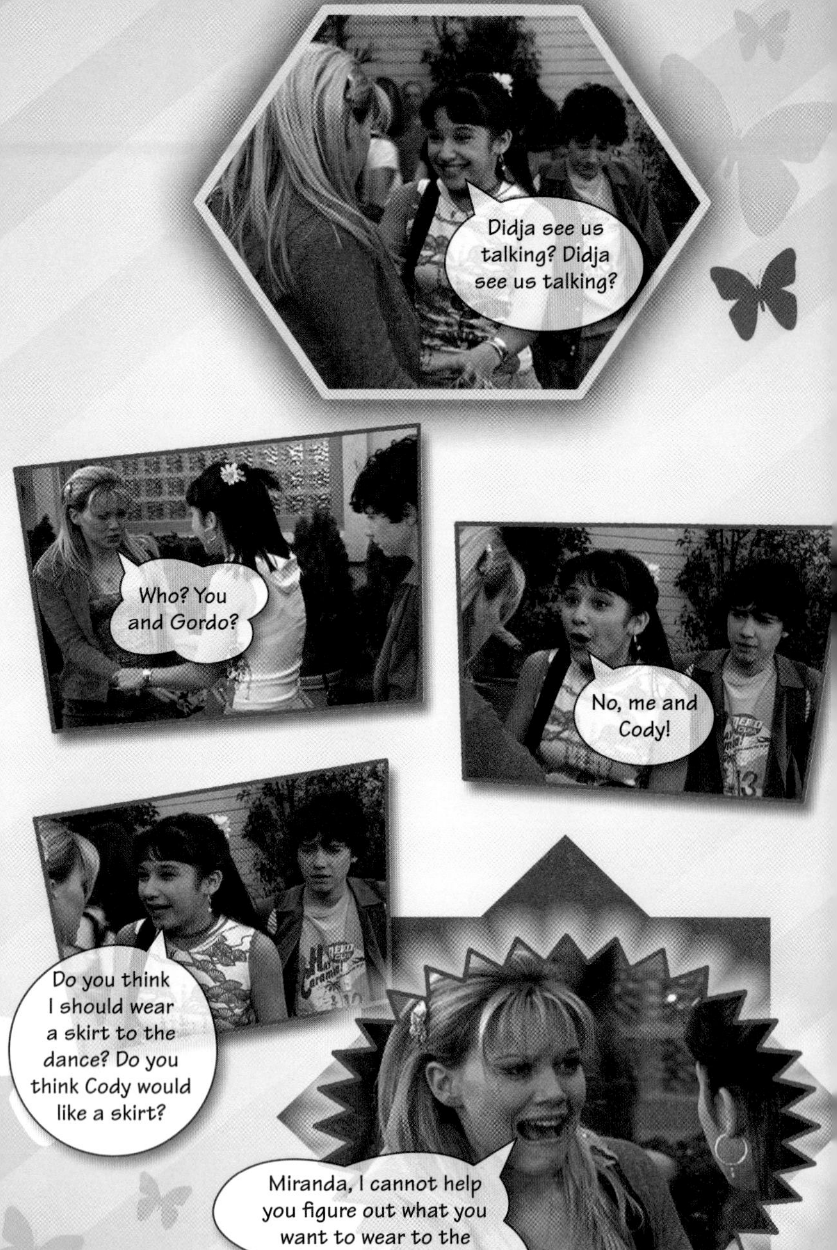
Didja see us talking? Didja see us talking?
Who? You and Gordo?
No, me and Cody!
Do you think I should wear a skirt to the dance? Do you think Cody would like a skirt?
Miranda, I cannot help you figure out what you want to wear to the dance right now. My stomach is in knots.

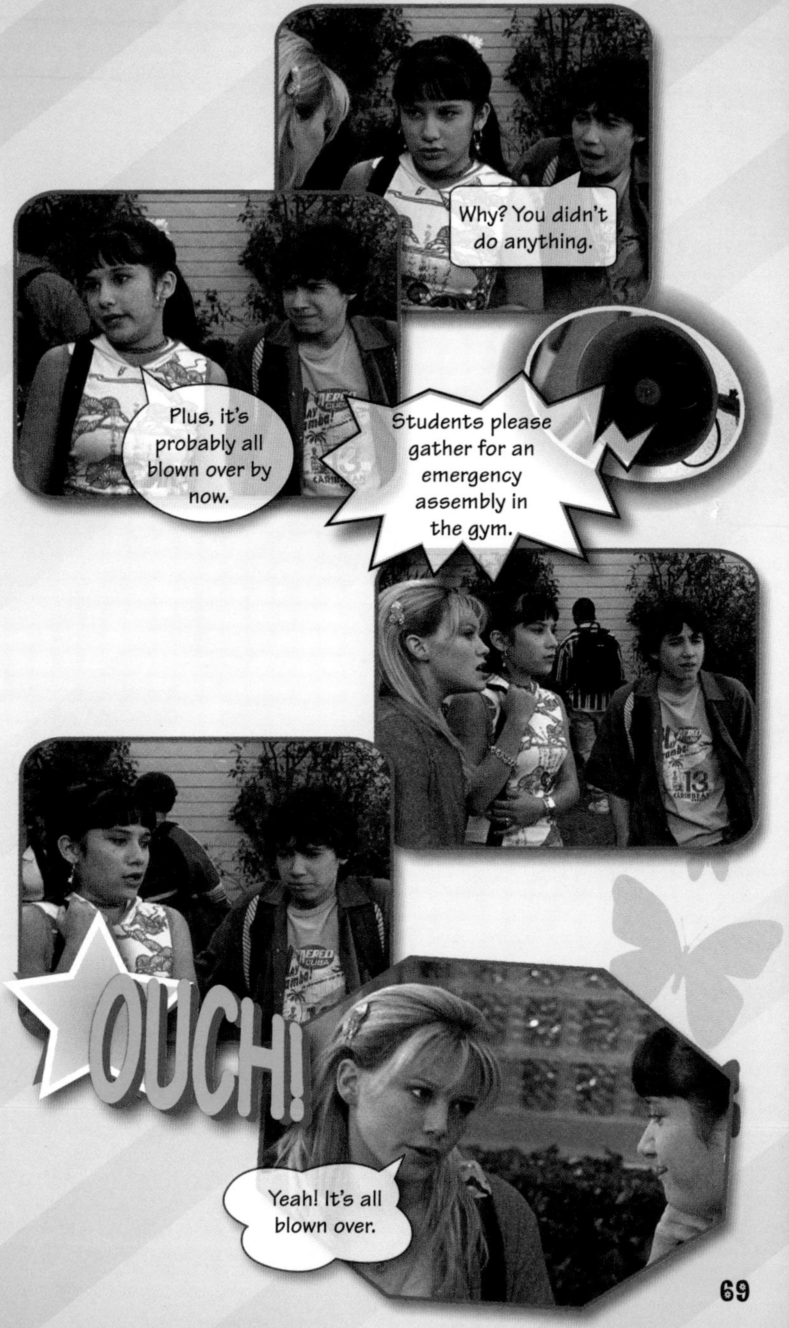
Why? You didn't do anything.
Plus, it's probably all blown over by now.
Students please gather for an emergency assembly in the gym.
OUCH!
Yeah! It's all blown over.

I've gathered the school because there has been an act of vandalism perpetrated in our little community.
You may feel that no one is affected, but you're wrong.
And we feel that someone here knows all about it.
The statue of our first principal has been defaced.

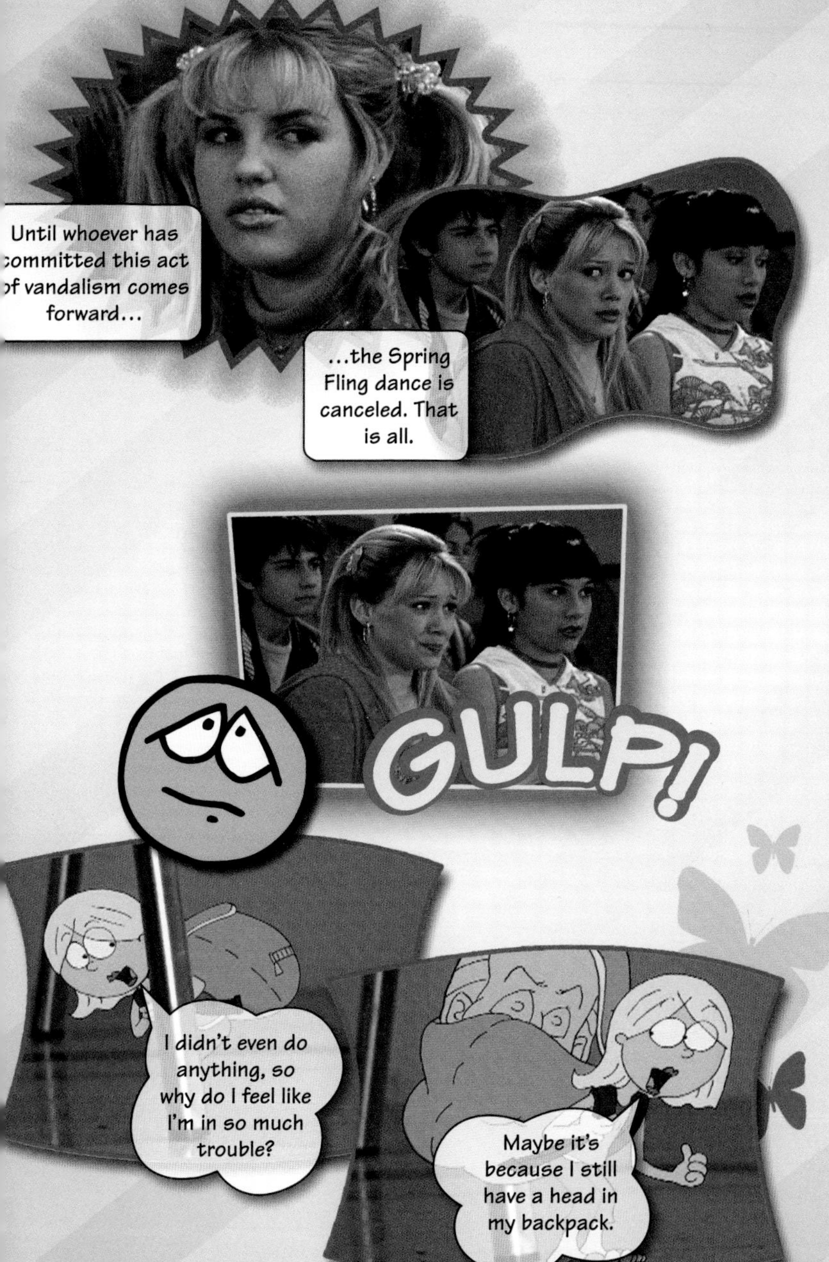

Until whoever has committed this act of vandalism comes forward…
…the Spring Fling dance is canceled. That is all.
GULP!
I didn't even do anything, so why do I feel like I'm in so much trouble?
Maybe it's because I still have a head in my backpack.

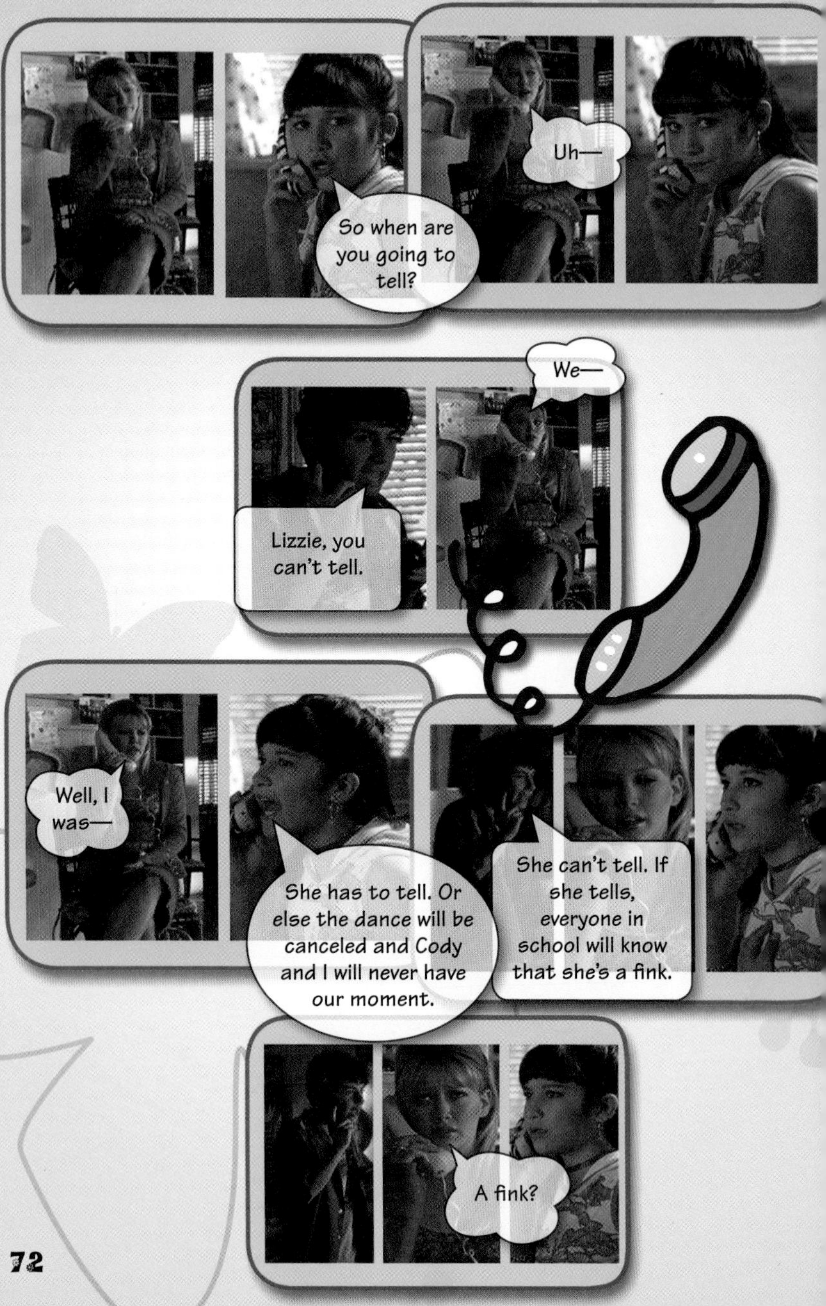
So when are you going to tell?
Uh—
We—
Lizzie, you can't tell.
Well, I was—
She has to tell. Or else the dance will be canceled and Cody and I will never have our moment.
She can't tell. If she tells, everyone in school will know that she's a fink.
A fink?

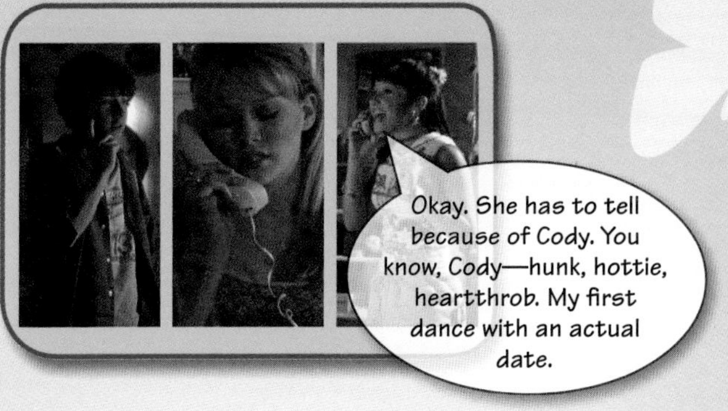
Okay. She has to tell because of Cody. You know, Cody—hunk, hottie, heartthrob. My first dance with an actual date.

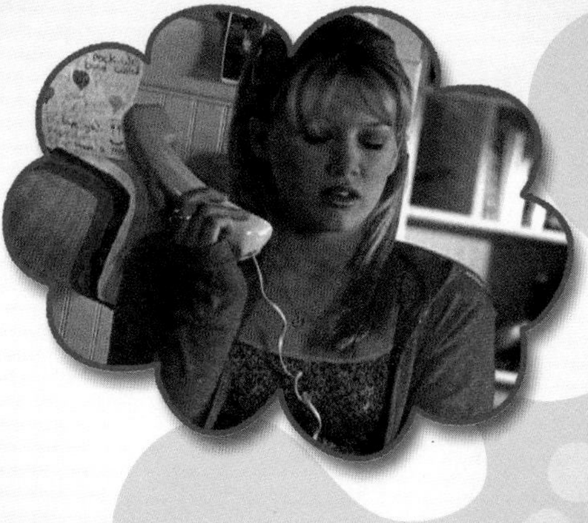

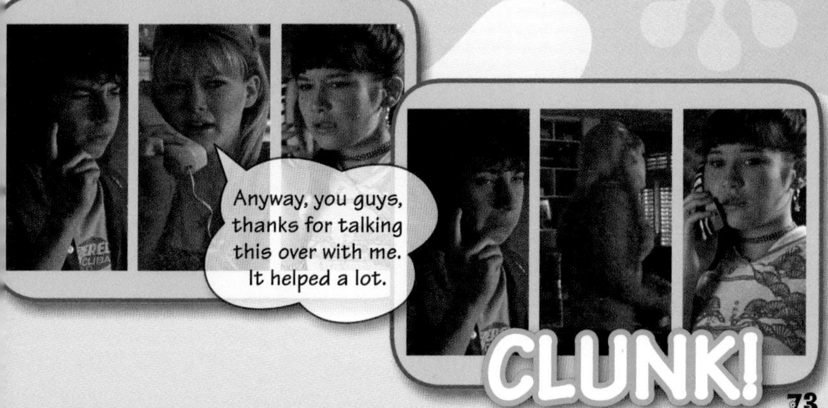
Anyway, you guys, thanks for talking this over with me. It helped a lot.
CLUNK!

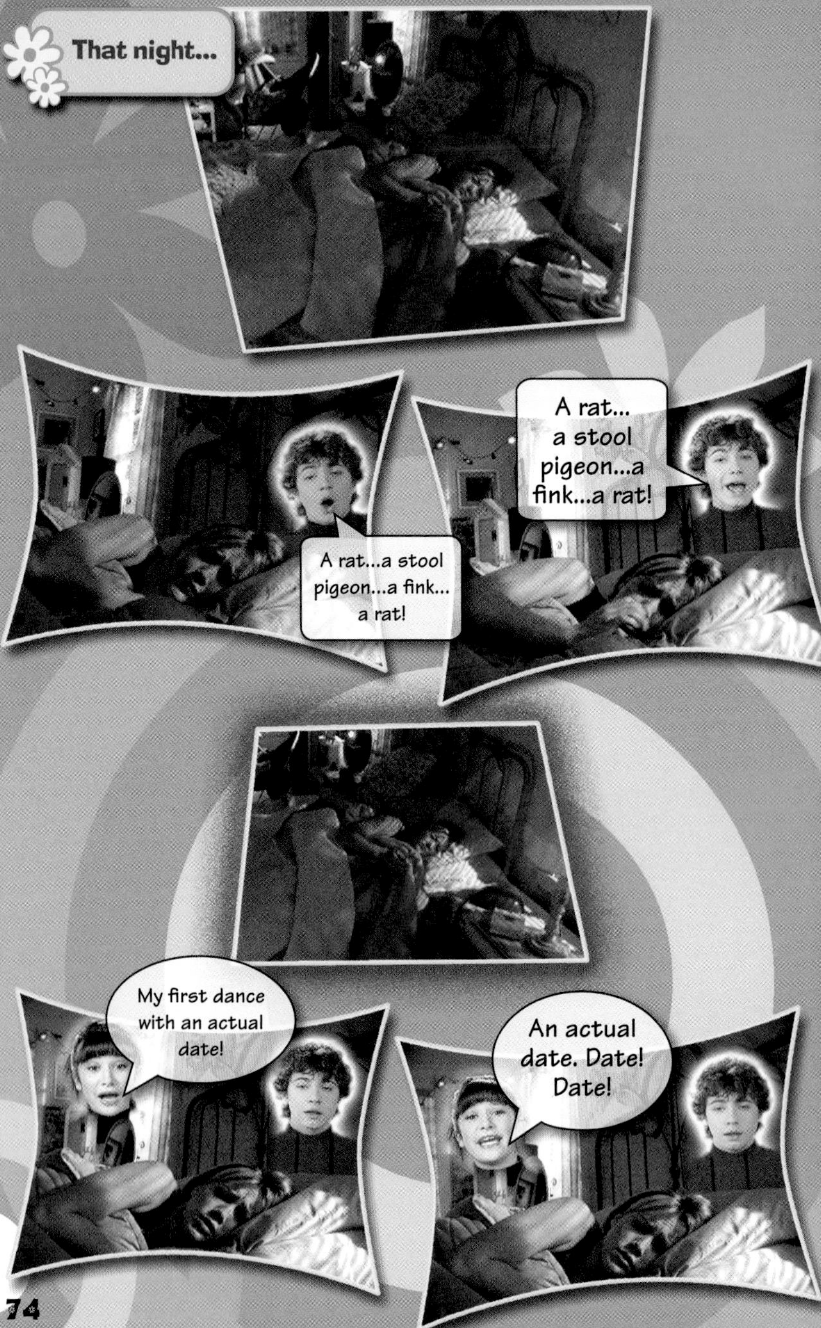
That night...
A rat...a stool pigeon...a fink... a rat!
A rat... a stool pigeon...a fink...a rat!
My first dance with an actual date!
An actual date. Date! Date!

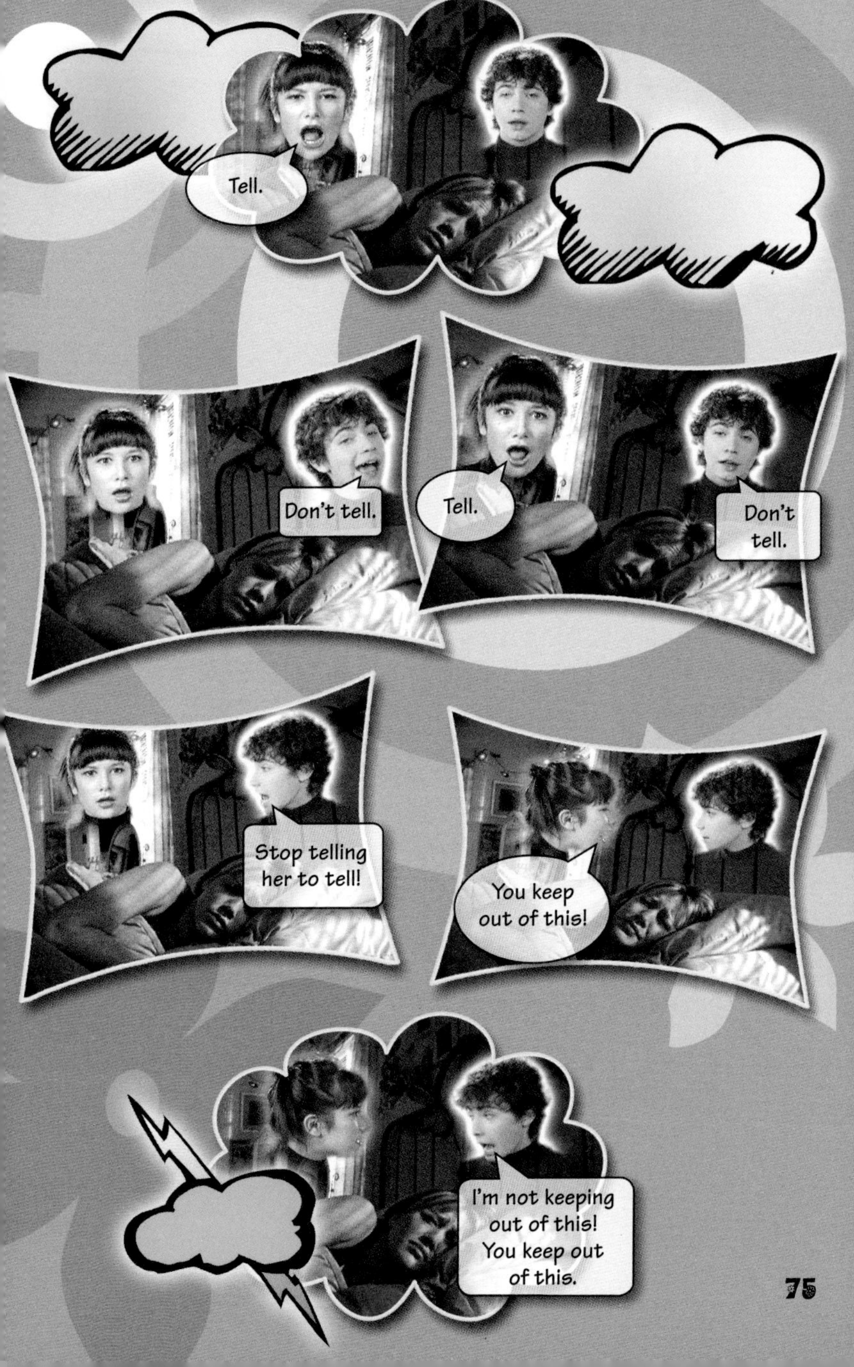
Tell.
Don't tell.
Tell.
Don't tell.
Stop telling her to tell!
You keep out of this!
I'm not keeping out of this! You keep out of this.

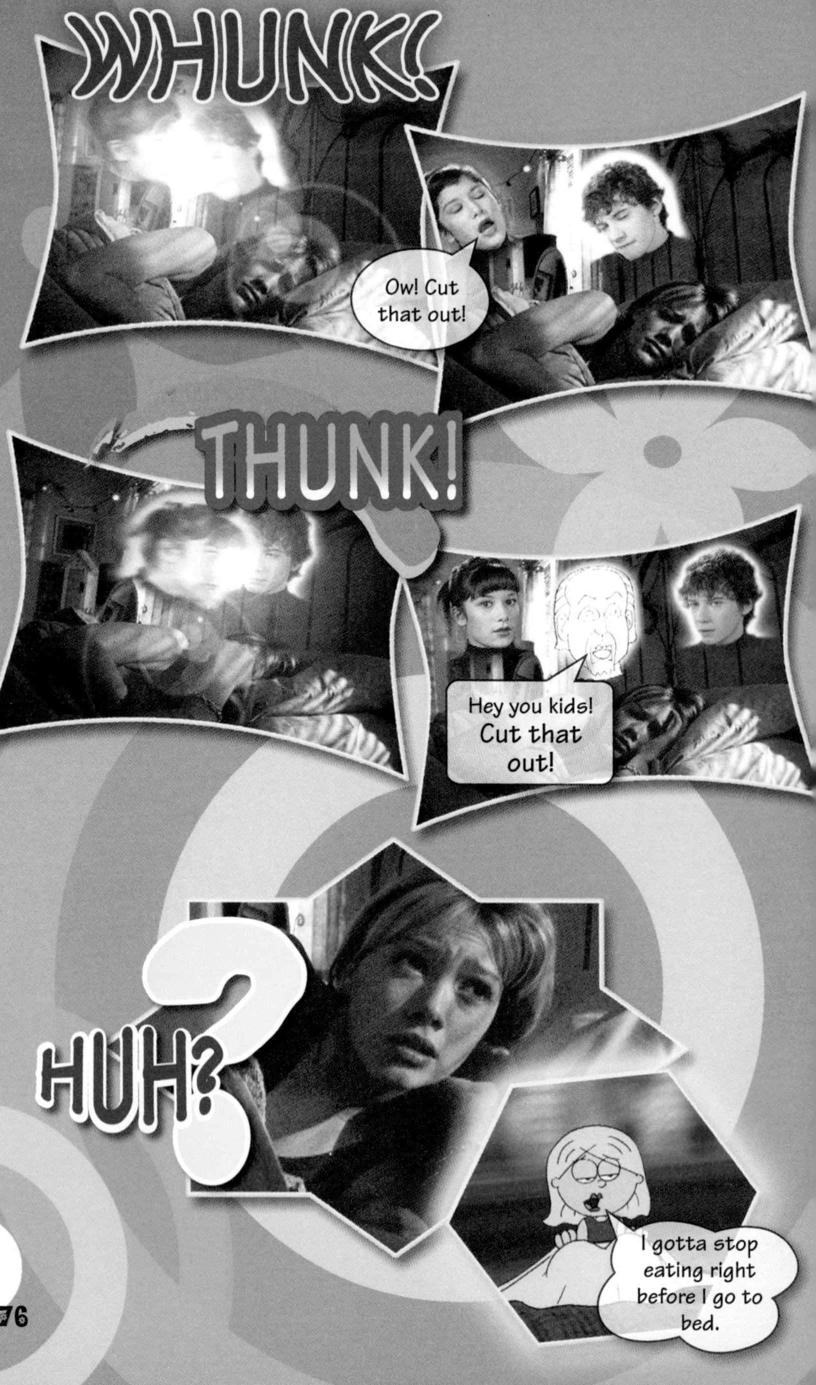
WHUNK!
Ow! Cut that out!
THUNK!
Hey you kids! Cut that out!
HUH?
I gotta stop eating right before I go to bed.

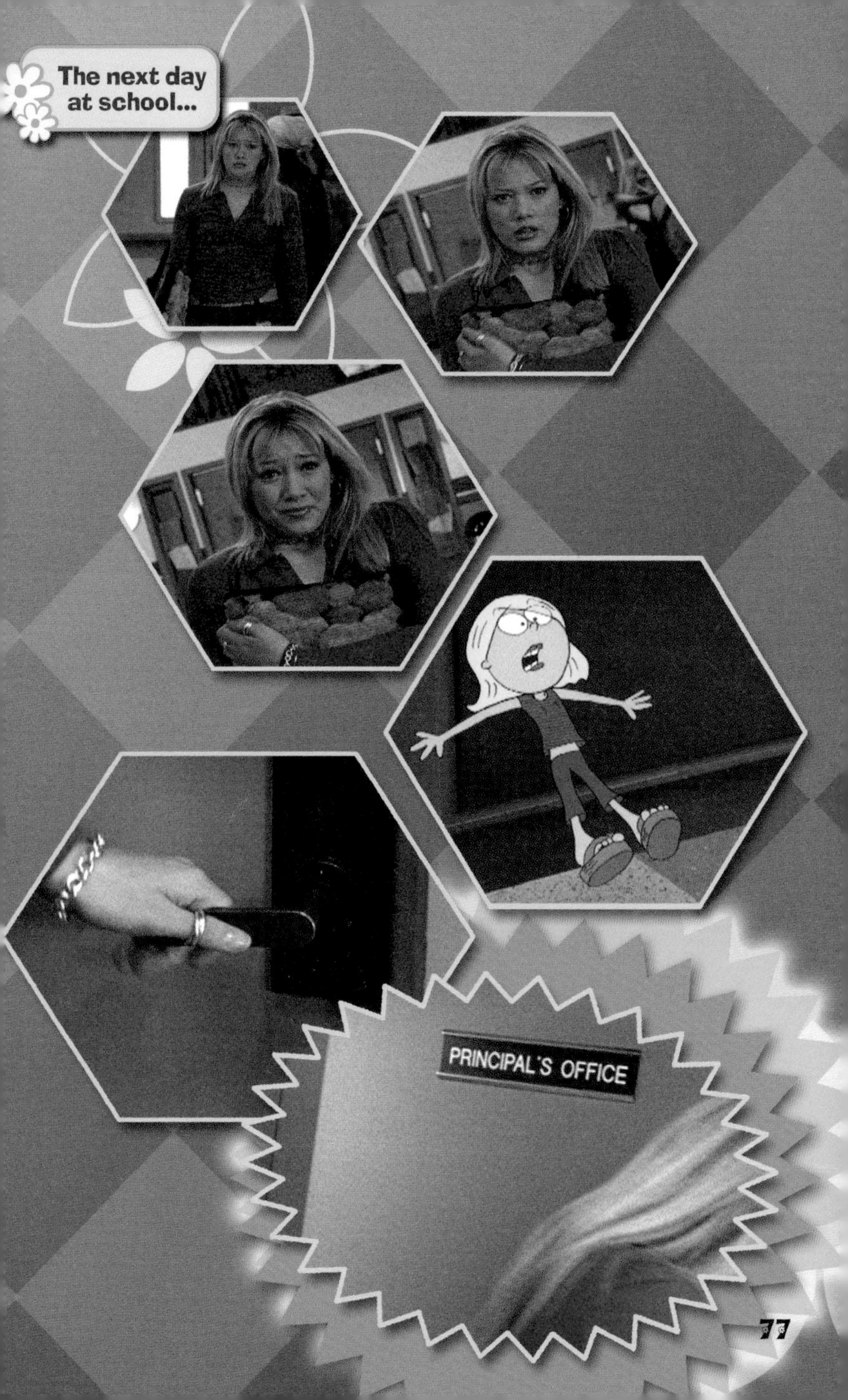
The next day at school...
PRINCIPAL'S OFFICE

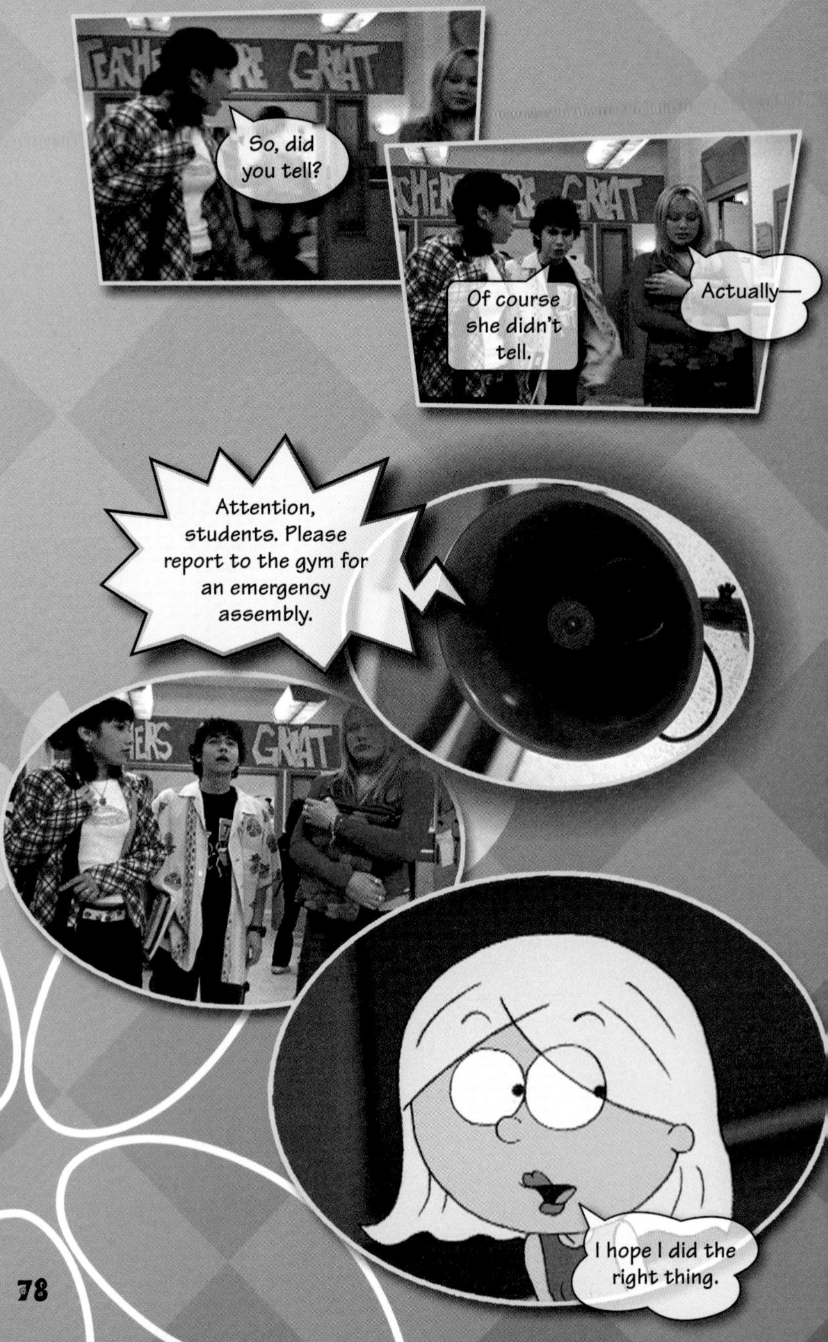
So, did you tell?
Of course she didn't tell.
Actually—
Attention, students. Please report to the gym for an emergency assembly.
I hope I did the right thing.

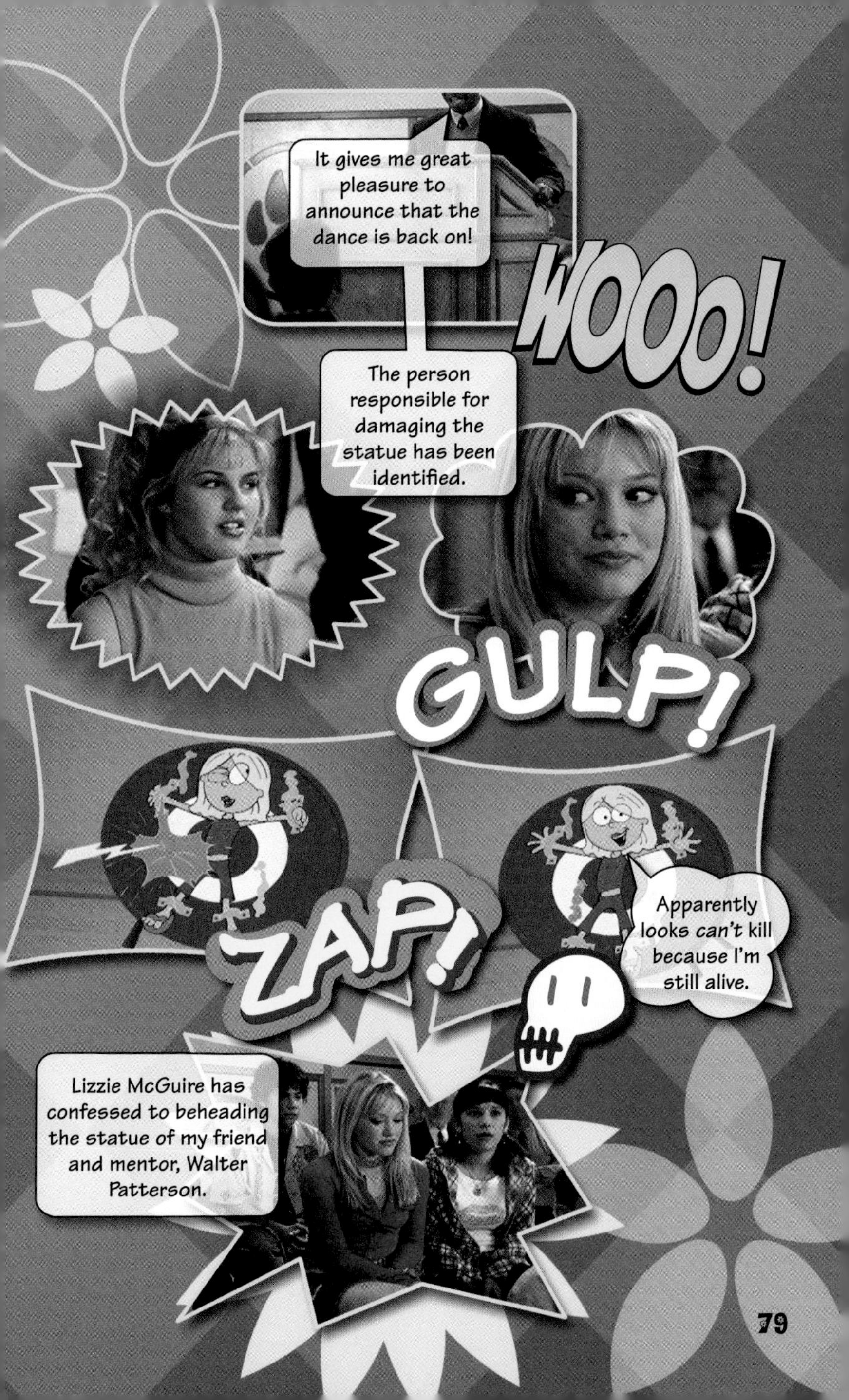
It gives me great pleasure to announce that the dance is back on!
WOOO!
The person responsible for damaging the statue has been identified.
GULP!
ZAP!
Apparently looks can't kill because I'm still alive.
Lizzie McGuire has confessed to beheading the statue of my friend and mentor, Walter Patterson.

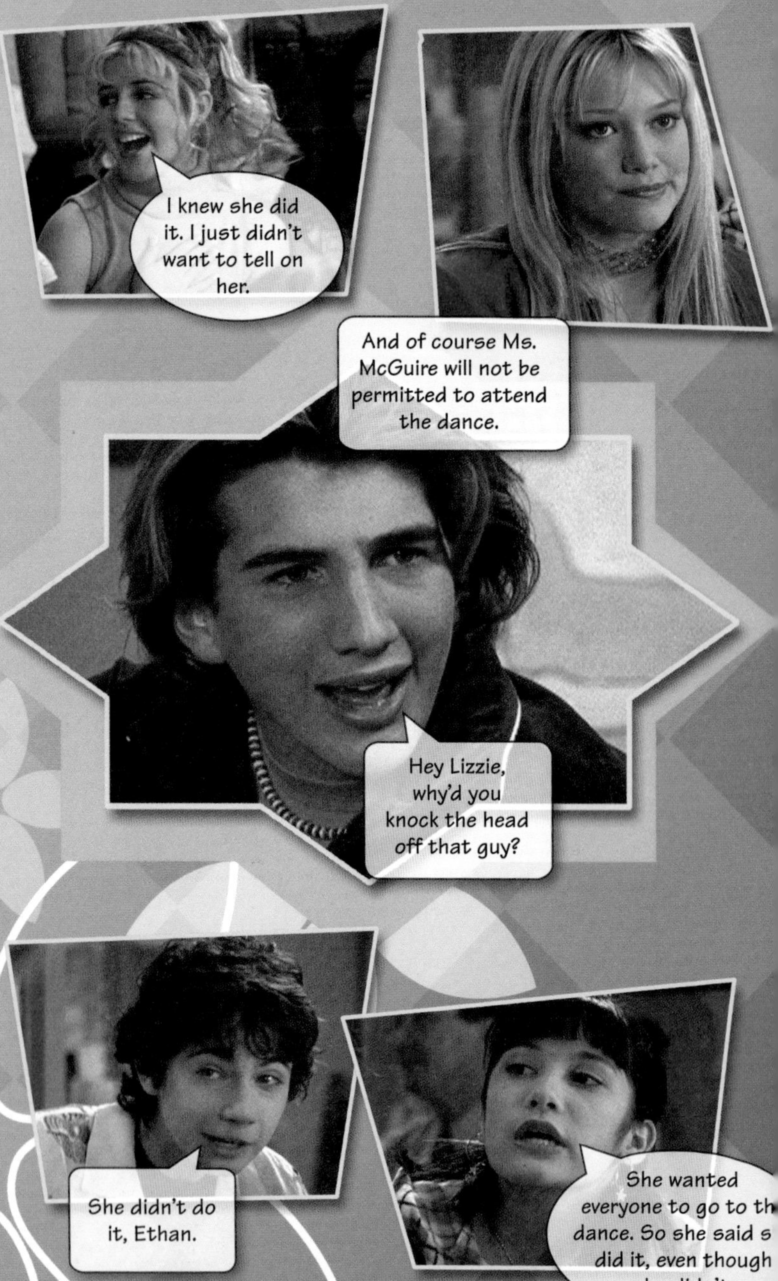
I knew she did it. I just didn't want to tell on her.
And of course Ms. McGuire will not be permitted to attend the dance.
Hey Lizzie, why'd you knock the head off that guy?
She didn't do it, Ethan.
She wanted everyone to go to th dance. So she said s did it, even though she didn't.

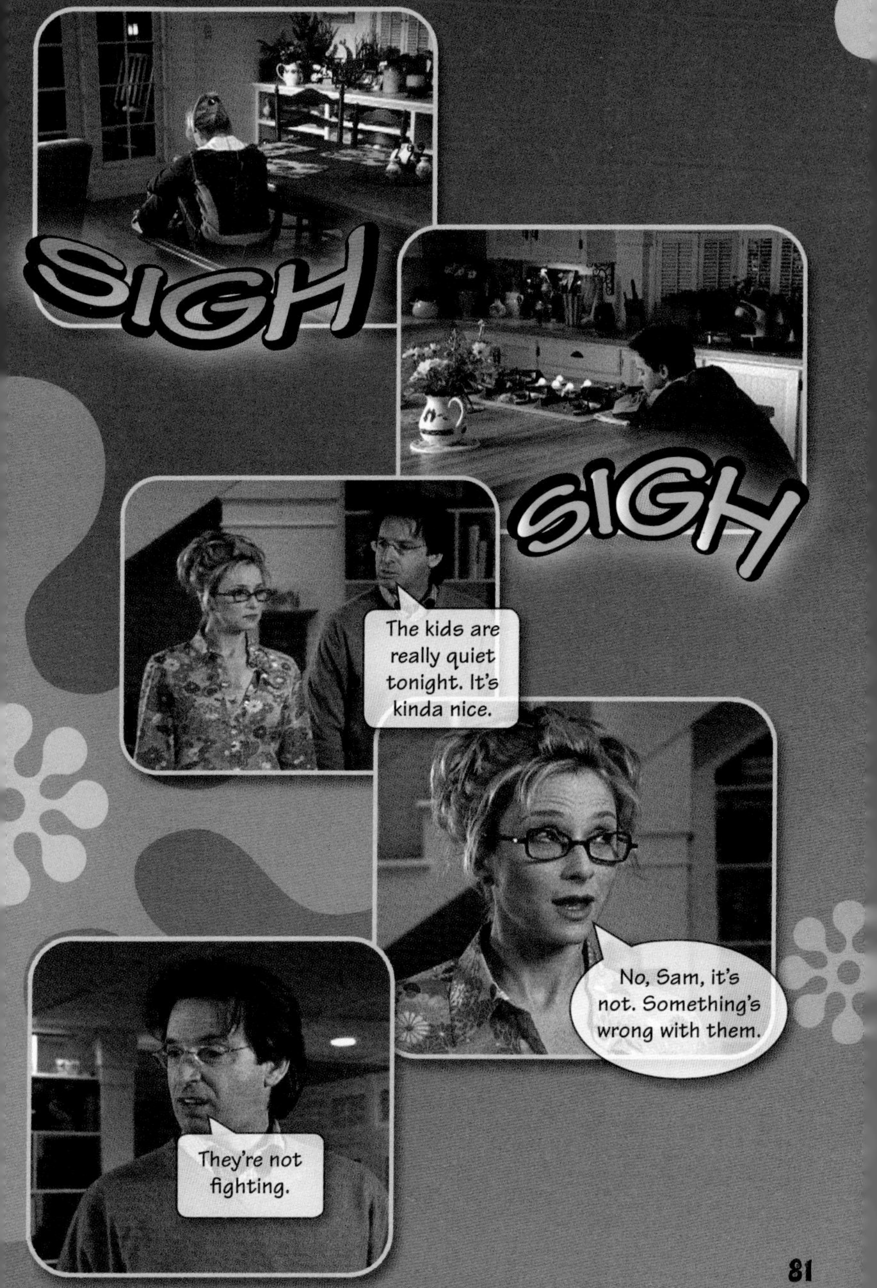
SIGH
SIGH
The kids are really quiet tonight. It's kinda nice.
No, Sam, it's not. Something's wrong with them.
They're not fighting.

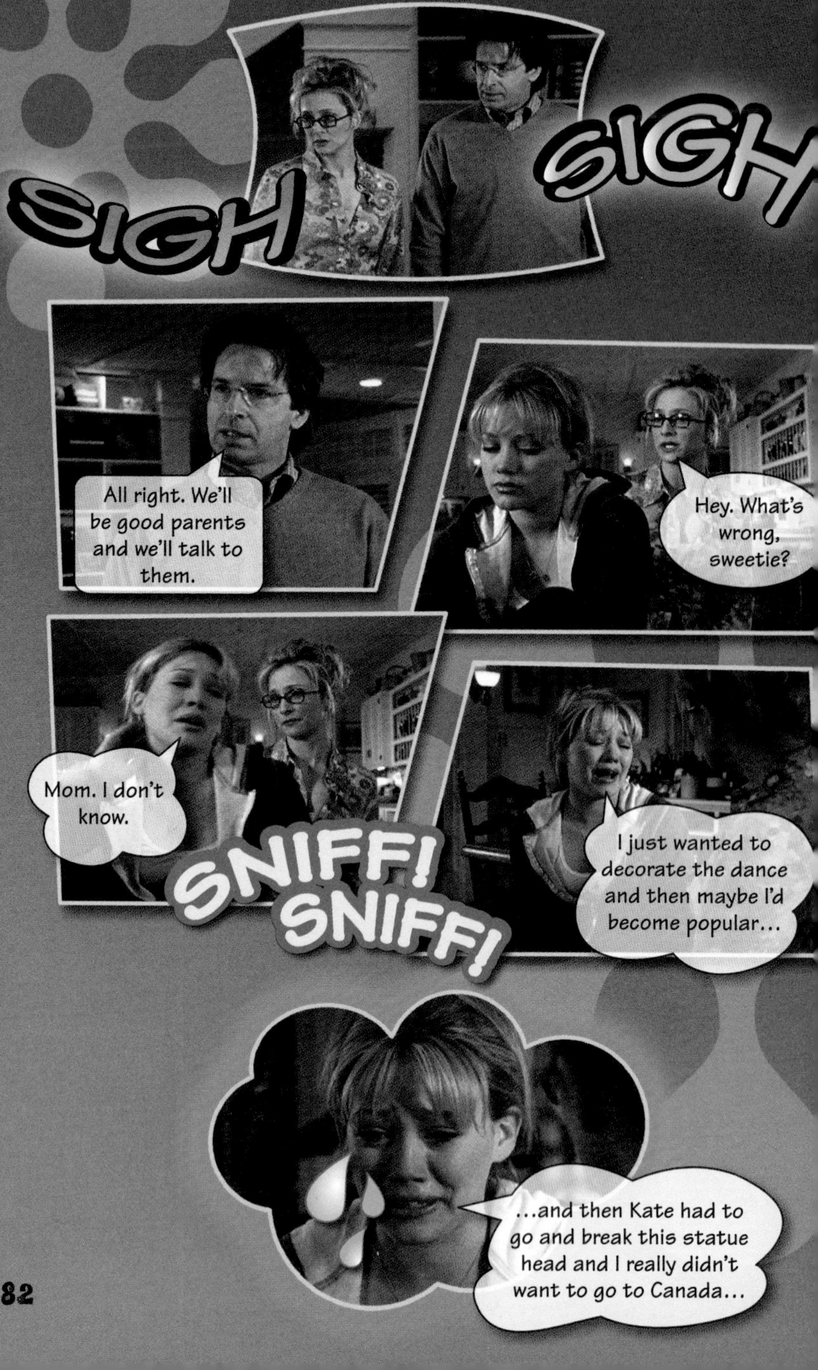
SIGH
SIGH
All right. We'll be good parents and we'll talk to them.
Hey. What's wrong, sweetie?
Mom. I don't know.
SNIFF! SNIFF!
I just wanted to decorate the dance and then maybe I'd become popular...
...and then Kate had to go and break this statue head and I really didn't want to go to Canada...

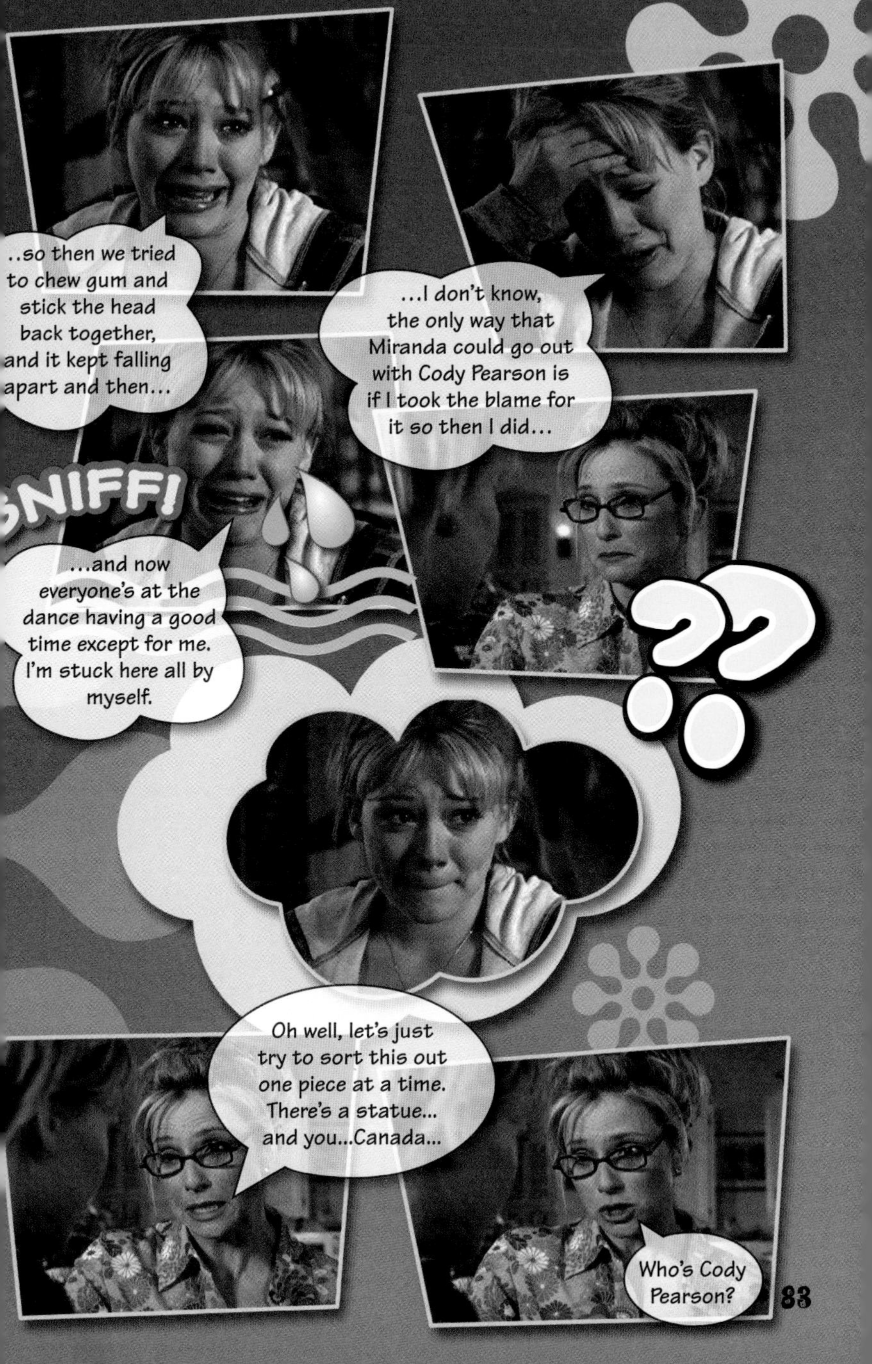
..so then we tried to chew gum and stick the head back together, and it kept falling apart and then...
...I don't know, the only way that Miranda could go out with Cody Pearson is if I took the blame for it so then I did...
SNIFF!
...and now everyone's at the dance having a good time except for me. I'm stuck here all by myself.
??
Oh well, let's just try to sort this out one piece at a time. There's a statue... and you...Canada...
Who's Cody Pearson?

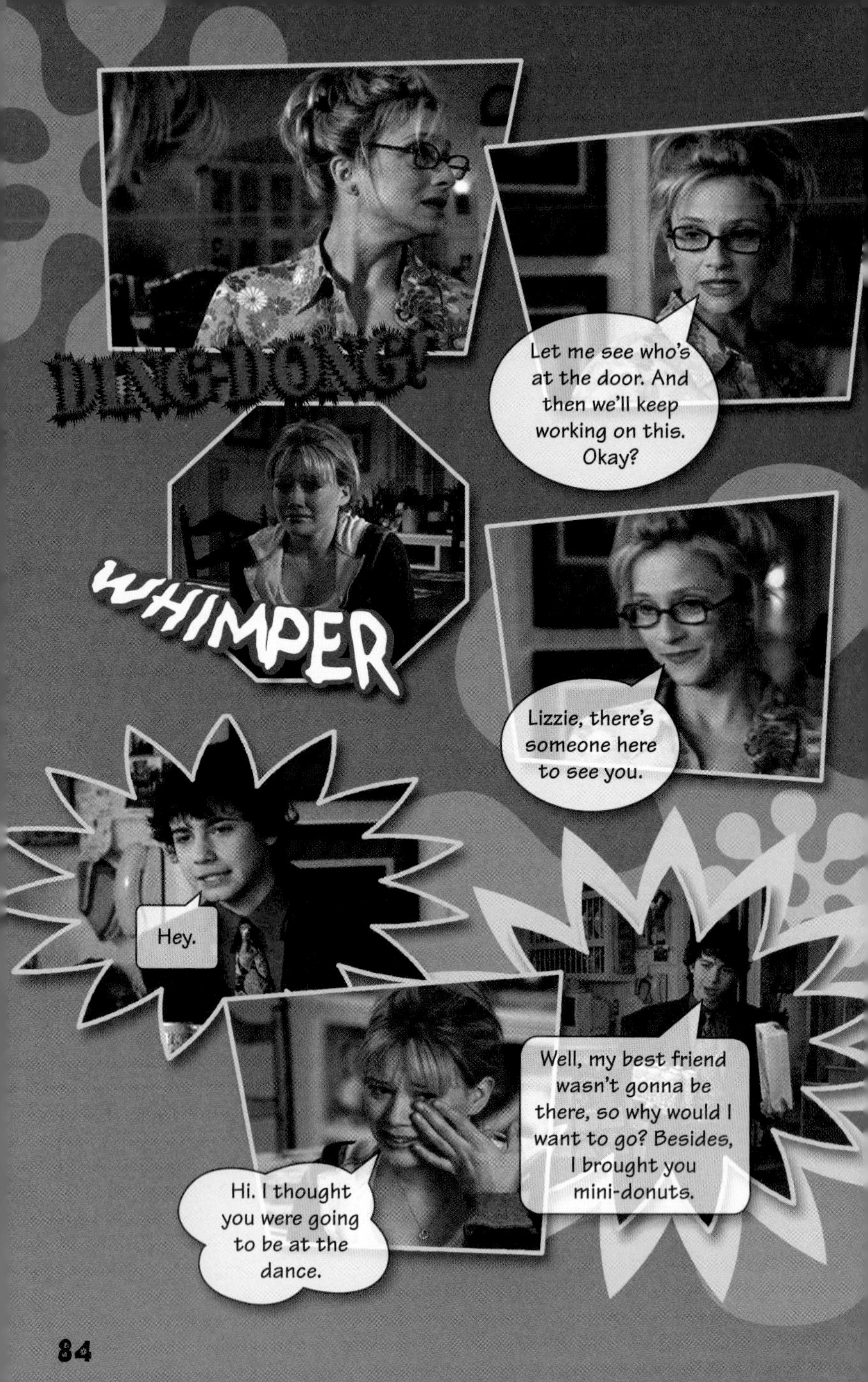
DING-DONG!
Let me see who's at the door. And then we'll keep working on this. Okay?
WHIMPER
Lizzie, there's someone here to see you.
Hey.
Well, my best friend wasn't gonna be there, so why would I want to go? Besides, I brought you mini-donuts.
Hi. I thought you were going to be at the dance.

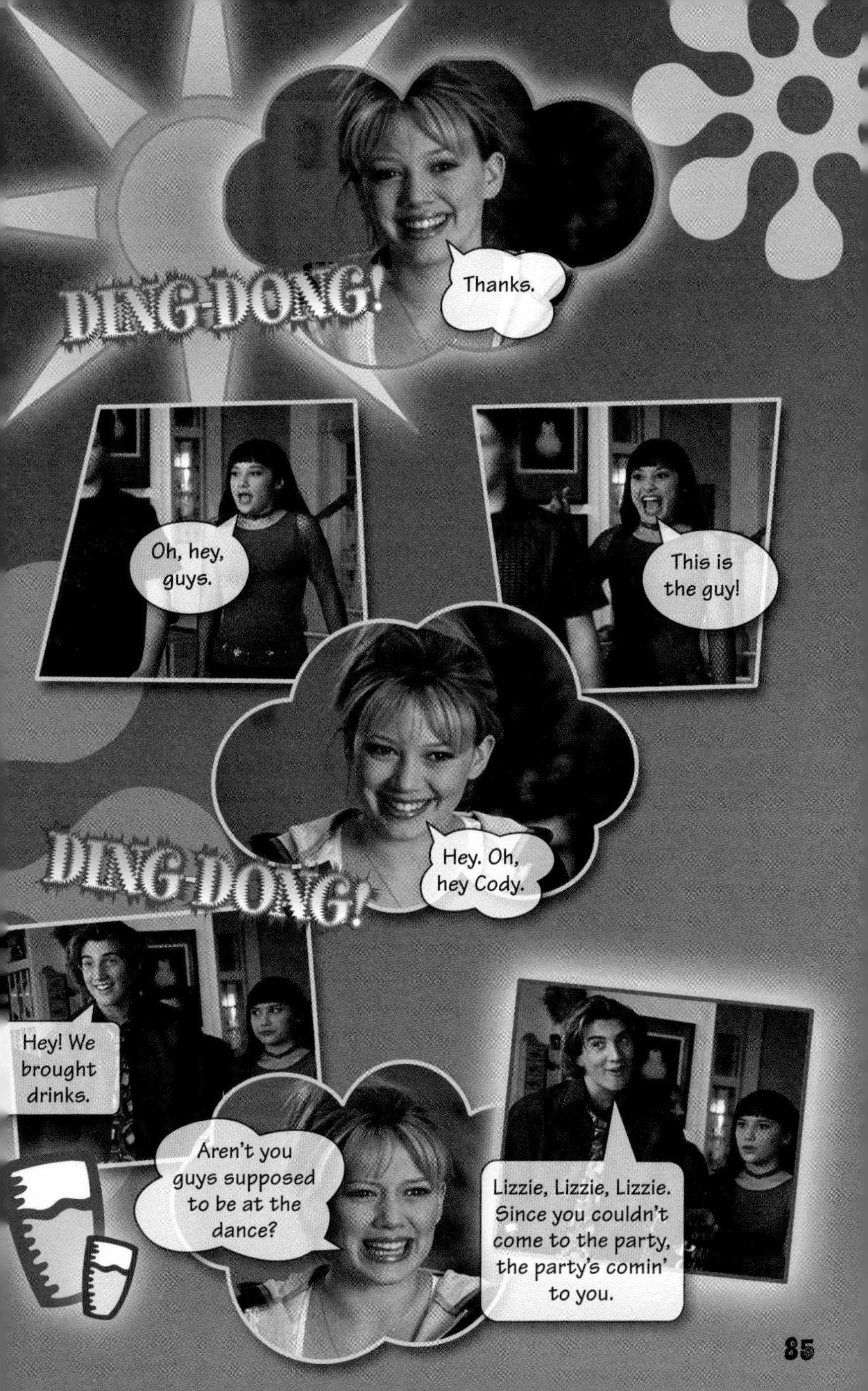

DING-DONG!
Thanks.
Oh, hey, guys.
This is the guy!
DING-DONG!
Hey. Oh, hey Cody.
Hey! We brought drinks.
Aren't you guys supposed to be at the dance?
Lizzie, Lizzie, Lizzie. Since you couldn't come to the party, the party's comin' to you.

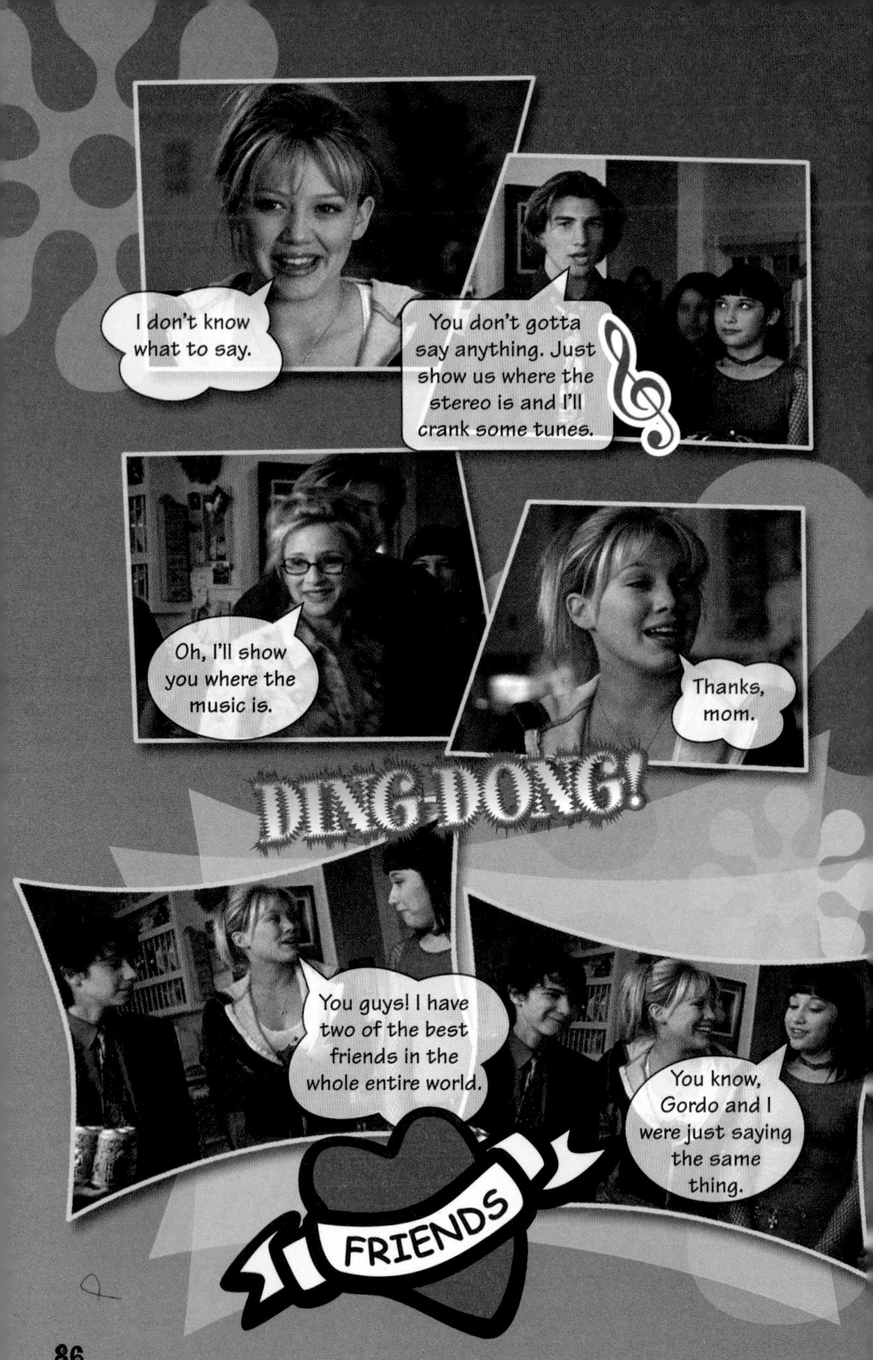
I don't know what to say.
You don't gotta say anything. Just show us where the stereo is and I'll crank some tunes.
Oh, I'll show you where the music is.
Thanks, mom.
DING-DONG!
You guys! I have two of the best friends in the whole entire world.
You know, Gordo and I were just saying the same thing.
FRIENDS

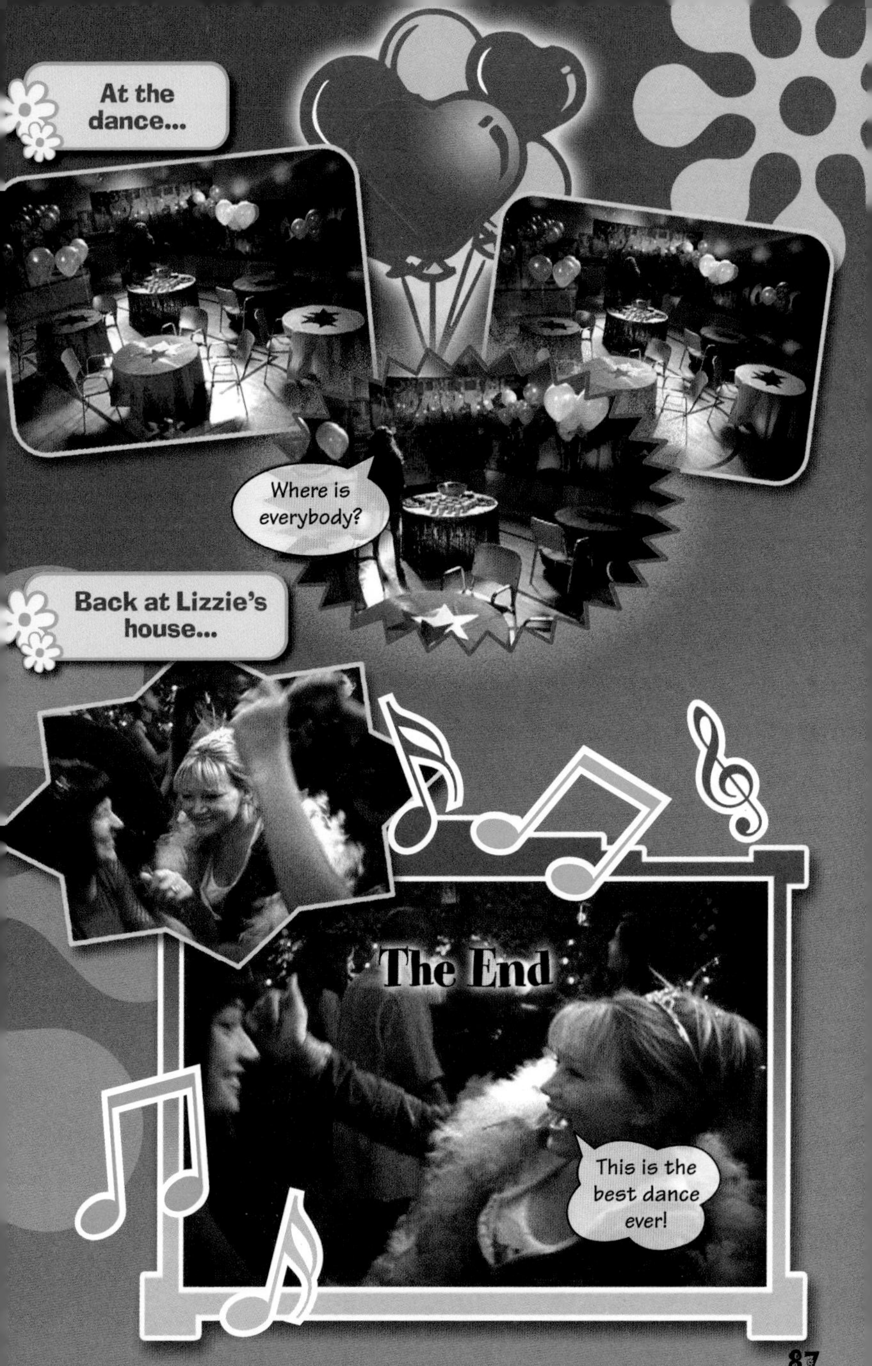
At the dance...
Where is everybody?
Back at Lizzie's house...
The End
This is the best dance ever!

Lizzie McGuire

CINE-MANGA™ VOLUME 9
COMING SOON FROM TOKYOPOP®

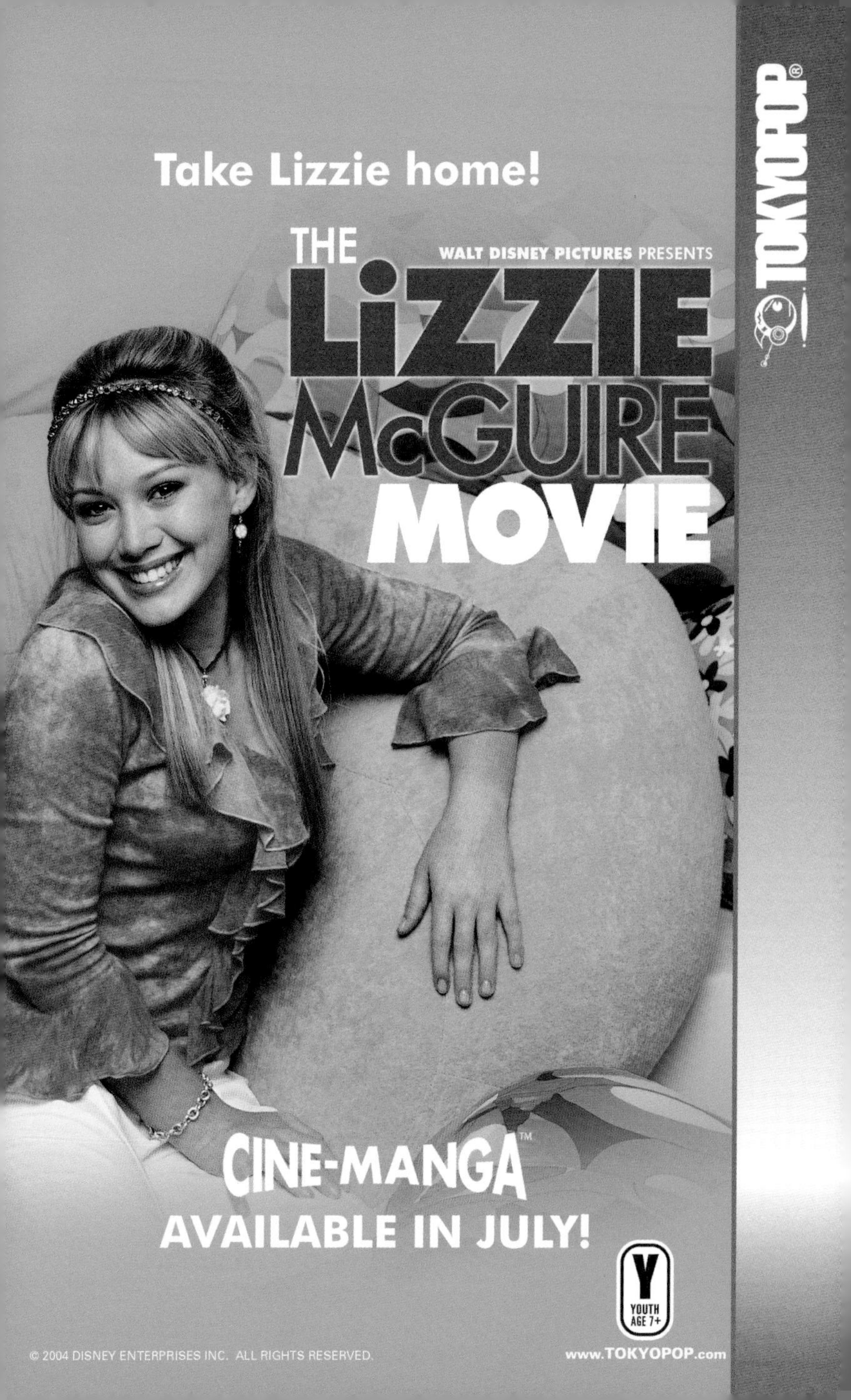
TOKYOPOP
Take Lizzie home!
WALT DISNEY PICTURES PRESENTS
THE LiZZIE McGUIRE MOVIE
CINE-MANGA™
AVAILABLE IN JULY!
Y YOUTH AGE 7+
© 2004 DISNEY ENTERPRISES INC. ALL RIGHTS RESERVED.
www.TOKYOPOP.com

ALSO AVAILABLE FROM ⊙TOKYOPOP®

06.21.04Y

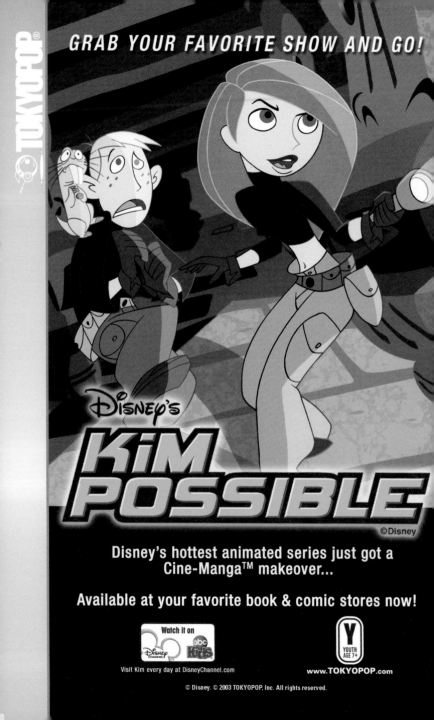

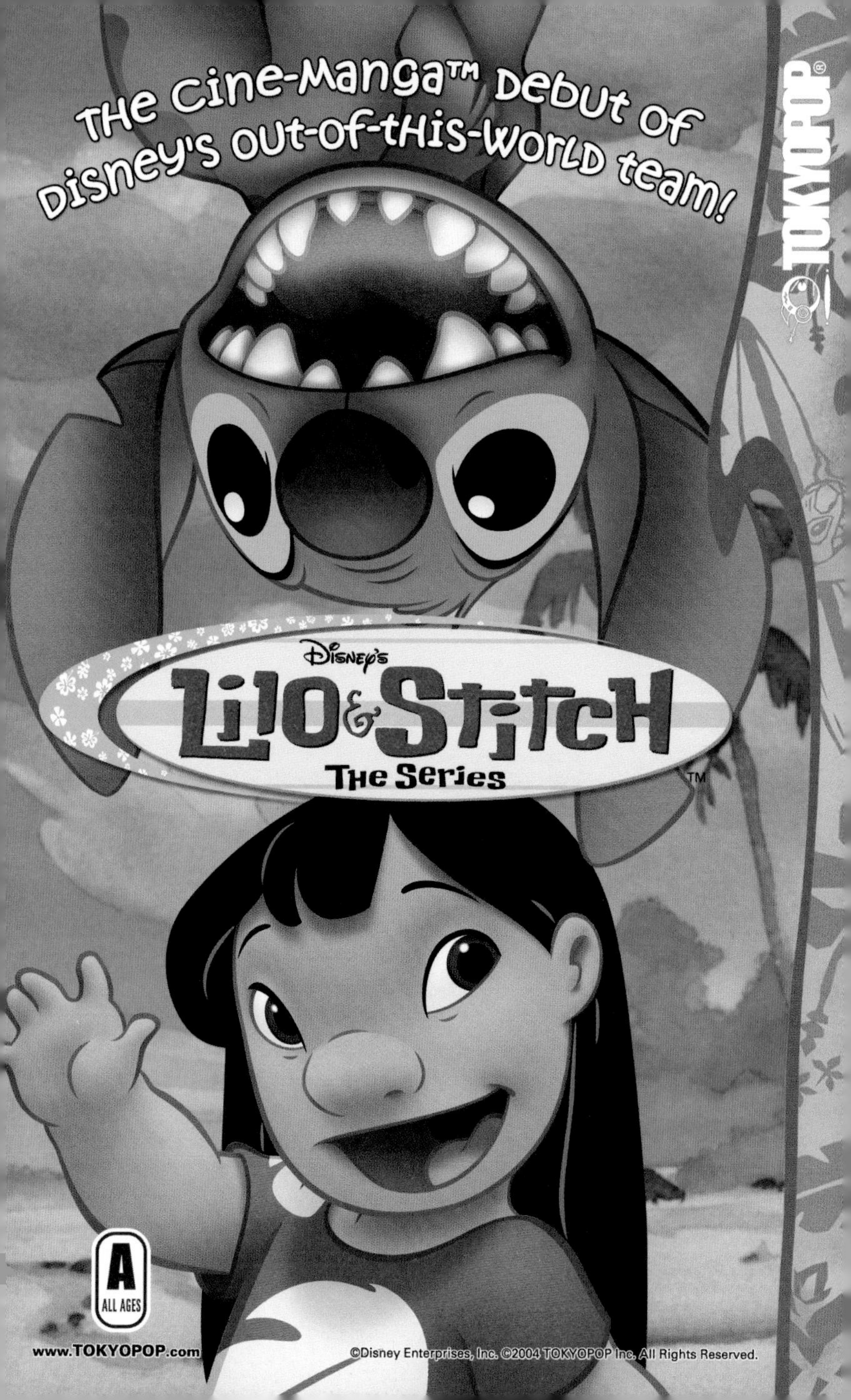
THE Cine-Manga™ DeBUt Of
Disney's OUt-Of-tHIS-WORLD team!
TOKYOPOP®
DISNEY'S
LILO & STITCH
THE SERIES™
A
ALL AGES
www.TOKYOPOP.com
©Disney Enterprises, Inc. ©2004 TOKYOPOP Inc. All Rights Reserved.

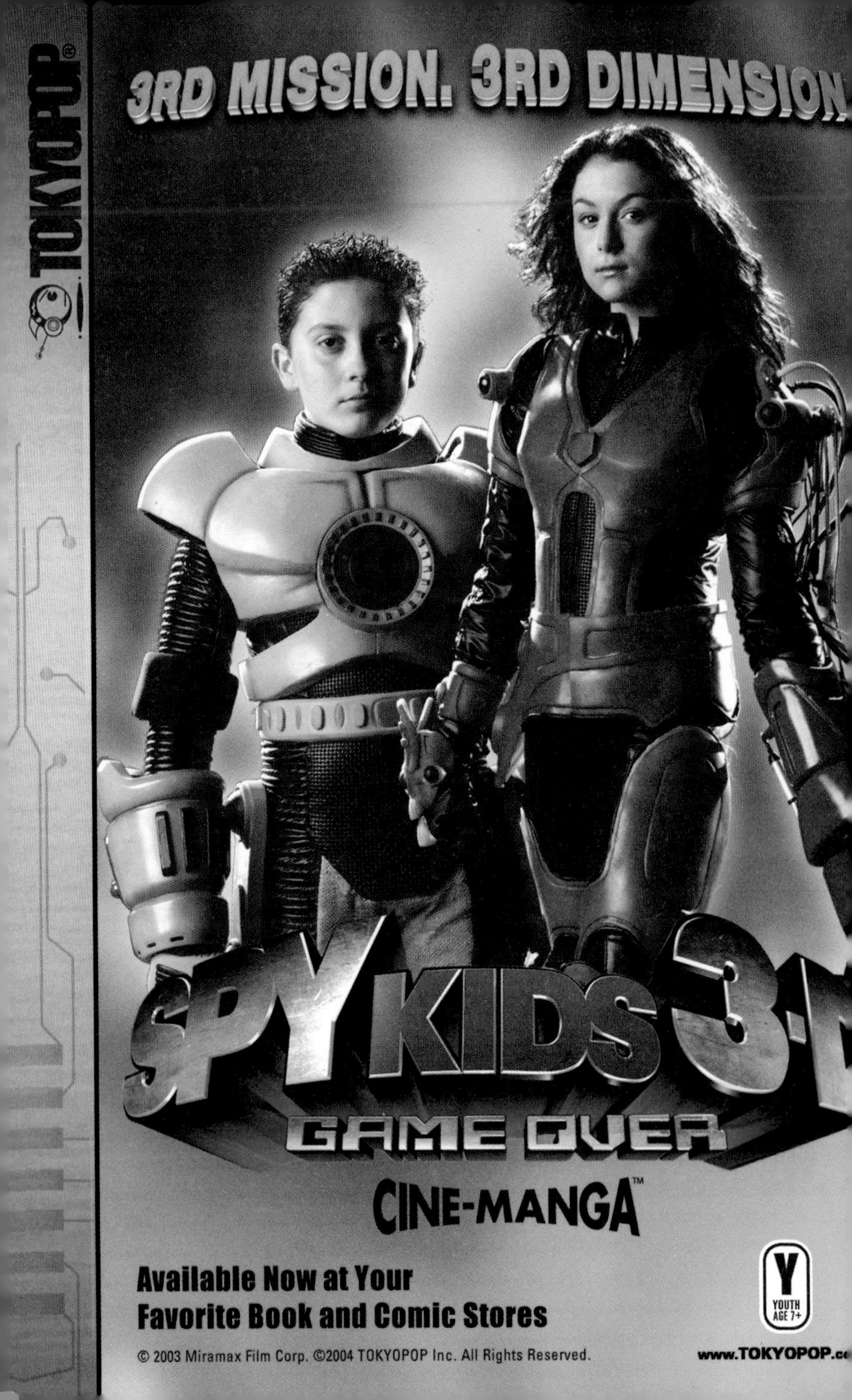
TOKYOPOP®
3RD MISSION. 3RD DIMENSION
SPY KIDS 3-D
GAME OVER
CINE-MANGA™
Available Now at Your
Favorite Book and Comic Stores
Y
YOUTH AGE 7+
© 2003 Miramax Film Corp. ©2004 TOKYOPOP Inc. All Rights Reserved.
www.TOKYOPOP.com

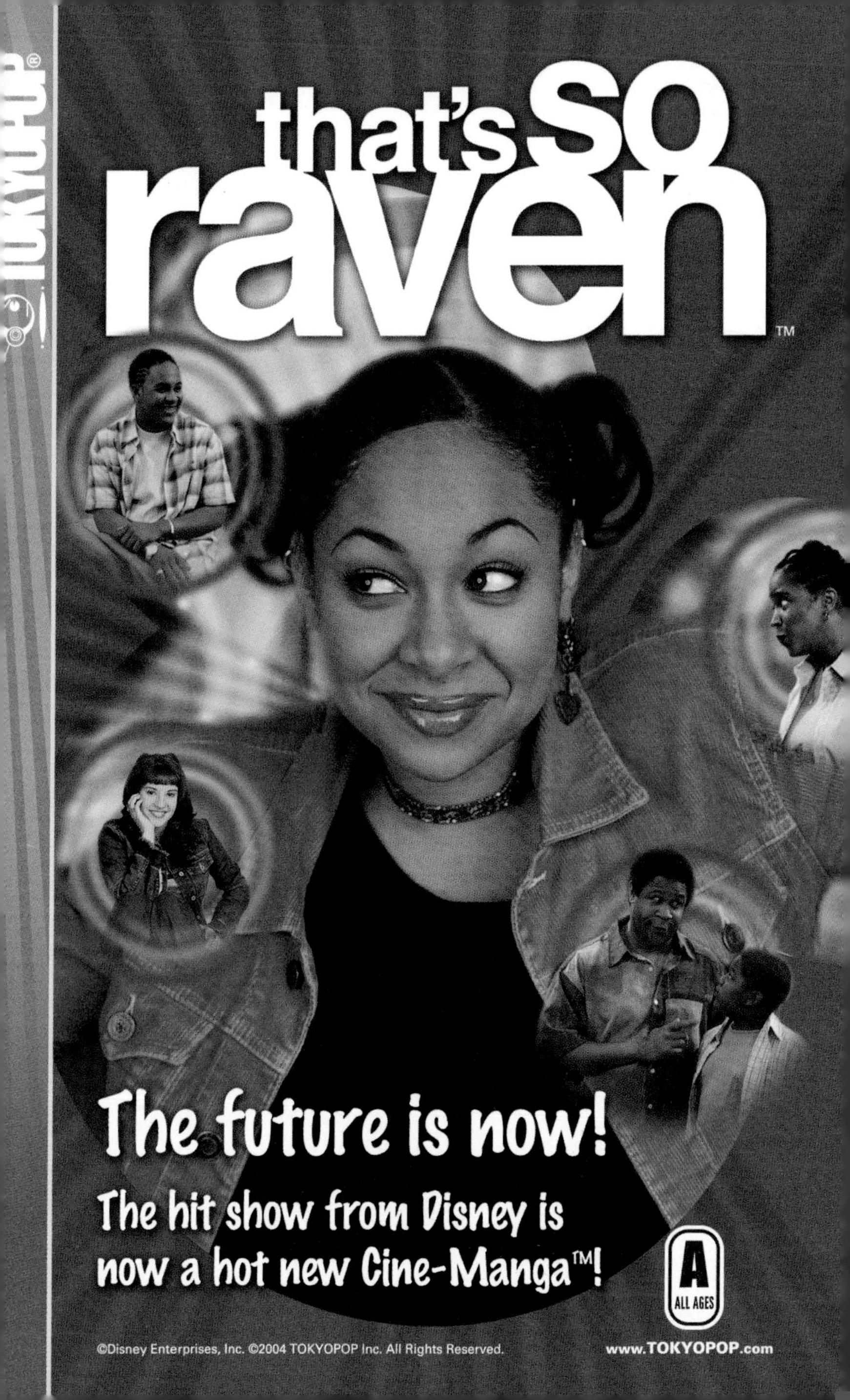

TOKYOPOP®
that's so raven™
The future is now!
The hit show from Disney is now a hot new Cine-Manga™!
A ALL AGES
©Disney Enterprises, Inc. ©2004 TOKYOPOP Inc. All Rights Reserved.
www.TOKYOPOP.com